FLOATING LUXURY

IWEIN MAASSEN

FLOATING

THE MOST LUXURIOUS CRUISE SHIPS

LUXURY

LANNOO

CONTENTS

FOREWORD

Cruising has become increasingly popular as more and more people are choosing to spend their holidays at sea. This is not without reason. The price/quality ratio is always favourable, and cruising is a unique experience, allowing those who live on the mainland to discover new horizons.

Leaving a place in the evening to then wake up the next morning at a new destination is really fascinating. Cruising is a voyage of discovery with the huge advantage that the hotel travels with you. You only have to unpack your suitcase once while you visit several places. During the day, you can explore a city or simply laze around on board, then sail again in the evening and enjoy the ship. And the next day, you pick a new destination — one could think of more boring ways to spend a vacation.

It is a misconception that cruising is for older people. The average age of first-time cruisers is under 40 because nowadays most ships are geared towards catering for children. Today, with such a wide range of cruises offered, it can be difficult to choose the right one.

This cruising book is intended to help you make the best choice. It provides helpful information about the top cruise ships currently available — 'La crème de la crème' of today's cruise industry. These are vessels that excel in the areas of service, food quality, décor, luxury, onboard entertainment, and more.

The ships are classified according to size, because size *does* matter. A week on a sailing yacht with 60 guests is a very different experience to a holiday on a ship with 3,000 passengers. The latter naturally has a wider range of leisure activities. All cruise ships aim to offer guests an enjoyable holiday, but it is important you choose a vessel that best suits your own personal needs.

This book will give you insight into a wide range of ships, but it is not exhaustive. It is intended to inspire, to be an eye-opener. Those of you who have not yet been on a cruise don't know what you are missing.

Happy sailing!

Iwein Maassen

BOUTIQUE SHIPS

XS

Of all the cruise ships, the boutique ships (with a maximum capacity of 250 guests) are the most intimate. This, of course, is due to their relatively small size. A boutique ship gives the impression of travelling on a private yacht rather than on a cruise ship. The staff not only knows your name; as soon as you appear at the bar, the barman will pour your favourite drink.

As these vessels have a shallow draft, they can travel to places that larger cruise ships cannot get to. Small, intimate harbours, remote bays and coves – it is destinations like these that often make a cruise memorable. Boutique ships have better moorings in large cities. In St. Petersburg, for example, it is easy to sail up the River Neva and moor at the quay close to the Hermitage while larger ships, because of their deep draft, have to dock about an hour away.

However, a very small cruise ship has its disadvantages. The captain of a European boutique ship once told me the story of a cruise that did not go so smoothly. An American company had rented half the cabins to thank its staff for a successful business year. The mood among the company's staff was boisterous and jolly, as is normal during staff outings.

This annoyed the other guests. The inappropriate behaviour of the Americans was seen as offensive. They appeared in T-shirts and shorts for the Captain's Cocktail, a festive champagne party around the swimming pool, with most of them drinking bottles of beer. The other guests (and the crew) had taken the trouble to dress formally...

Tall boutique vessels are the finest of all cruise ships. These are elegant sailing ships, such as the imposing five-master, the Royal Clipper, the largest sailing ship in the world. A cruise on a sailing ship is a different experience from a cruise on a normal ship. There is an atmosphere of togetherness on board and travellers who book this kind of cruise are generally athletic types, often people who own or have owned a sailboat or who are interested in the art of sailing. Passengers have the option to help on board, but it is not mandatory. On some ships, passengers can even take the helm (under supervision, of course) – an experience that men, in particular, do not want to miss. The captain usually gives a detailed explanation of the manoeuvres he makes with his ship, normally in a relaxed manner on the outside deck in the morning sun.

On a sailing ship, you become much more aware of the elements because you rely on the wind in order to sail. However, if the elements are not favourable, the ship can always run on her engine. On a tall ship you are closer to the sea, literally. Anyone who has ever stretched out in the net under the bowsprit while dolphins swim around and jump out of the water will have to agree that this is an unforgettable experience.

And then there is the silence when you are sailing. No droning of an engine, just the sound of the wind and of the bow cutting through the sea.

SEA CLOUD

Built as a private yacht at the beginning of the last century, the Sea Cloud is now in service as a luxury cruise ship. This 109-metre-long yacht is still largely in its original state, though it has been adapted to modern-day requirements. The history of this lady of the sea reads like an exciting book.

Built in Germany in 1931 as the largest private yacht at that time, the four-masted barque was purchased by E.F. Hutton, a successful American businessman on Wall Street. The ship, with her black hull, was christened 'Hussar' and Hutton's wife, Marjorie Merriweather Post, concentrated on the interior. This fabulously wealthy heiress of a large American food production group spent more than two years working on this task full-time. She set about the work with zeal; she had the cabins reconstructed in their actual size at a warehouse in Brooklyn to enable her to complete the interior step by step before everything was shipped to the vessel. The antique furniture, paintings and other treasures were selected with the greatest care for the seven cabins. These rooms maintain many of the original details to this day. On account of its commercial function, the ship was extended to include a superstructure and now has a total of 32 cabins. In addition to the 60-man crew, she can also accommodate 64 passengers.

The couple sailed the Hussar frequently, both for business and for pleasure. But unfortunately, the marriage hit the rocks in Augustus 1935. Knowing just how much she was attached to the yacht, Ed Hutton gave it to his former wife the day after their divorce. Majorie accepted

it gladly and, in order to herald a new era, she renamed the vessel 'Sea Cloud'.

Four months after her divorce, she married her childhood friend, Joseph Davies. He was a lawyer and a diplomat, and when he was appointed Ambassador to the American Embassy in Leningrad (now St. Petersburg) at the beginning of 1937, he took his wife and the yacht with him.

The Sea Cloud served as a kind of floating palace where important guests were received. The threat of war meant that the vessel had to make a detour to return to the United States. Following the Japanese attack on Pearl Harbour, America was at war and, as a result, the American navy requisitioned various yachts in order to deploy them as warships. However, President Roosevelt, who was a good friend of Davies and knew the Sea Cloud well, refused to call up the sailing yacht for military service because he considered her to be too nice for that purpose.

Nevertheless, in 1942 the time finally came. The ship was painted grey, stripped of her masts, equipped with guns and leased by the United States for the symbolic amount of one dollar per year. Under the code name IX-99, she served as a weather station in the Azores and near Greenland. But luck was on the side of the ship because she was one of the few private yachts to come through the war. Not intact though, as the luxury interior had suffered greatly during the presence of the military. A military decoration can still be seen on the bridge comprising five chevrons, one for each half-year that the Sea Cloud served in the American navy.

In 1949, the yacht, now painted white, served again as a reception facility for the Davies couple. Then, when Joe and Marjorie's marriage suffered a crisis in the early fifties, Marjorie decided to sell the vessel. Maintaining the ship (there were 72 crew members alone) had become too much for her.

In 1955, she sold the Sea Cloud to the Dominican dictator, Rafael Leonidas Trujilo Montinas. The ship was renamed 'Angelieta' and was mainly used for private purposes. When Trujilo's son, Ramfis, went to study in San Francisco, he took the yacht with him to serve as accommodation. In those days, the yacht featured in the tabloid news almost weekly on account of the infamous parties thrown by the young student. Stars like Zsa Zsa Gabor and Kim Novak were regular guests at these events.

Trujilo was murdered in 1965 and a revolution broke out in the Dominican Republic. The new rulers were not interested in the yacht. To remove the blemish of the dictator, they renamed her 'Patria' and put her up for sale. It took five years before the American John Blue, owner of Operation Sea Cruises, bought the vessel. The 'Patria' was rechristened 'Antarna' and underwent total restoration in Naples. There were problems with the American tax authorities and the yacht was detained in Miami on her return in 1968. And there she remained for eighteen months until Charles and Stephanie Gallagher set eyes on her.

Stephanie wanted to start an 'Oceanic School' where students could, in addition to their normal studies, gain experience of other cultures, languages and scientific research. The students would also form the crew. Stephanie entered into an agreement with John Blue to lease the 'Antarna'. However, ambiguities in the contract led Blue to refuse to let the yacht leave port. Stephanie ignored this order, nevertheless, and she, together with 90 students hijacked the 'Antarna' As a joke, they even hoisted the Jolly Roger to the top of the mast! John Blue was not amused and had the vessel detained – yet again – in Panama, where it remained neglected for eight years. without anyone looking after it.

The sailing yacht, then in very poor condition, was eventually spotted by a German captain, Hartmut Paschburg who convinced a few German businessmen to buy the yacht. Emergency repairs were made to enable the vessel (which has since regained her old name) to cross the ocean. In October 1978 the Sea Cloud moved to Hamburg where it was restored to her former glory and adapted to the requirements of the time.

The Sea Cloud embarked on her first commercial cruise at the end of 1979 and since then, the elegant lady of the sea has once again been admired on the world's oceans. The ship now has room for just 64 guests and 60 crew members.

SILVER EXPLORER

Of all the cruises on offer, the expedition cruise is the most adventurous, particularly when the voyage takes passenger to remote regions, such as Antarctica. Those that seek adventure but don't want to give up their creature comforts and luxury should consider a cruise on the Silver Explorer.

Just about everyone has seen them, the black and white photographs of rugged men who had to endure the most extreme weather conditions during an expedition to Antarctica. The pictures of the 1914 trek, under the leadership of Shackleton, are particularly impressive. During that voyage, the sailing ship 'Endeavour' got stuck in an ice floe and was eventually smashed into matchwood by drift ice. After 20 months and many hardships, the 27-member crew was finally rescued. This was certainly a dangerous and heroic expedition, but nowadays a voyage to Antarctica can be undertaken in a much more luxurious and safer way.

In the world of expedition cruises there are various ships offering fabulous voyages. At the top end of the market there are only a few vessels that guarantee an abundance of luxury and comfort, whether during a cruise around the Galapagos Islands or to Spitsbergen. Hapag Lloyd's Bremen and the Hanseatic expedition ships and the National Geographic Orion are very popular and offer cruises around Australia and Indonesia as well as to Antarctica.

And then there is the Silver Explorer. This vessel was commissioned in 1989 as the Prince Albert II and subsequently joined the Silversea fleet in 2008 after being completely refitted. The small, manoeuvrable ship carries 132 passengers and 111 crew members, has suites only (all with a sea view), as well as butler service and 24-hour room service. To guarantee a good night's sleep, guests can choose from nine different types of pillow. Champagne, wine and spirits are served free of charge throughout the day and the minibar in the suite is filled daily according to the guest's wishes. The atmosphere on board is informal, and the service is excellent and inventive. What about serving champagne and strawberries dipped in chocolate after arriving in Antarctica... in a Zodiac on the way back to the ship!

Expedition cruises through the Caribbean, along the coast of Africa, Greenland or Canada are all on the programme. Those wanting to discover even more can also book an onshore stay before or after the cruise via Silversea.

Thanks to a reinforced hull (the ship has the High Ice Class 1A for passenger vessels in the Lloyd's Register), the Silver Explorer can navigate effortlessly through the Arctic and Antarctic, the ultimate mecca for expedition ships. The differences between the two extremities of the world are huge, which means that a cruise in one of these regions is a completely different experience. While Antarctica is a continent surrounded by ice, the North Pole (the Arctic), is an ocean surrounded by continents. The North Pole is only one meter above sea level, whereas the average height of Antarctica is 2,180 metres. There are no land mammals living in Antarctica, only marine mammals. In addition to the marine mammals living in the Arctic, there are reindeer, wolves, polar bears and foxes.

The average temperature at the North Pole is −18° C, significantly higher than at the South Pole, where the average temperature is −50° C.

Drake Passage, 17 November. On the way to Antarctica! This morning at 5.30 a.m., everyone was on deck to spot the first icebergs. Wow! Some look more like floating tower blocks while others have the freakish form of an abstract sculpture. Really bizarre, it seemed like we were on the set of a science fiction film about sailing. The sky was blue and the sun was shining brightly but the biting wind was icy cold. I didn't feel it because I was so in awe of the bizarre, surrealistic natural phenomena. Once back inside, the steaming coffee soon warmed our hands and nose... Looking forward to tomorrow, when we ride the Zodiac to go ashore in Paradise Bay!

The Silver Explorer is equipped with modern high-tech systems to guarantee the safety of the passengers. The environment is also treated with great care. There is an extensive expedition support team on board during the cruise. Biologists, geologists, botanists, ornithologists, as well as film makers specialising in nature documentaries, give talks on the regions visited.

A nature discovery tour is an experience in itself. Combined with the comfort and service of a luxury ship like the Silver Explorer, an entire collection of unique and unforgettable memories is guaranteed. Truly an undefeatable combination.

ANTARCTICA

For a long time, Antarctica was an unexplored region. It was not until the beginning of the 19th century that people began to take an interest in this icy continent. It is now a spectacular cruise destination.

It was only when seal hunter William Smith reported a large seal population on the South Shetland Islands in February 1819 that interest in this region began. There was a lot of seal hunting in those days and people were curious to know what lay behind the islands off the west coast of the Antarctica Peninsula. This aroused interest in Antarctica and the challenge to reach the South Pole was born. It was the records and diaries of polar explorers such as Scott, Shackleton and Amundsen that gave the continent its identity. The advent of photography also enabled people to view and take interest in this relatively undiscovered area of the earth.

It was eventually the Norwegian, Amundsen, who was the first to reach the precise point of the South Pole on 14 December 1911. The Englishman, Scott, was also on his way there at the same time. But Amundsen was much more efficient. With reindeer skin clothing and well-trained huskies, he reached the South Pole eight days sooner than planned. Scott, who was travelling with a larger group of people and ponies, was just behind. The ponies sank into the snow and eventually had to be killed. This meant the explorers had to pull the sledges with the supplies themselves. They finally reached the South Pole only to discover that Amundsen had already planted the Norwegian flag. Disillusioned, they turned around. But winter had set in and they were no longer able to reach their base camp. All the men froze to death.

Antarctica is now the most southerly destination that can be reached by a cruise ship. And it is probably the most spectacular. The region is larger than Europe and the lowest temperature ever on earth was measured here: minus 92.2 degrees Celsius. Approximately 90% of the earth's fresh water resources are found here: if all the ice in Antarctica were to melt, the sea level around the entire globe would rise by 85 metres. The cliffs and the permanent ice on that continent cover an area of 14 million sq. kilometres in summer, with the surface area doubled in winter by the formation of ice. Cruise ships can only reach the region between November and March during the Antarctic summer. Typically, only landings on the Antarctic Peninsula (via Zodiac) are offered, though there are also some ships that sail exclusively along the Antarctic coast and do not offer any landings. Despite its extreme remoteness, around 36,000 people visit the icy continent each year.

The 1959 Antarctic Treaty provides permanent monitoring of the region. The twelve countries that signed the Treaty, including Belgium, want to prevent Antarctica from becoming a victim of any future conflict between the superpowers. The Treaty bans military activities, rejects any claim to land (by all countries) and guarantees unhindered access for scientific research.

STAR FLYER

Those who want to experience the romance of a bygone age and who love freedom, wind and sailing, would be wise to take a cruise on a tall ship like the Star Flyer.

You would think that the rich and famous in Monaco would be well used to the high-tech ships and boats that flaunt themselves in the sun. But it is an old-fashioned sailing ship that steals the show here. When the Star Flyer hoists her sails, people get up from their terrace chairs and pull out their cameras to watch with bated breath. The sails catch the wind and billow and the ship starts to move noiselessly, gracefully turning its stern towards the coast.

Watching the Star Flyer is fun, but naturally, being on board is even better. Mikael Krafft, owner of the Star Clippers shipping company, to which the Star Flyer belongs, is amused as he looks towards the quay, leaning nonchalantly over the railing. 'Well, they are seeing something fantastic, of course. They are looking at the past. A tall ship under full sail like this four-master exudes nostalgia and romance; you can't compare it with anything else. Isn't that much more impressive than a modern luxury motor yacht?'

However, this ship lacks nothing in luxury. As old-fashioned as the 111-metre clipper might look, it is actually very modern. The ship, christened in 1991, is fully equipped with all possible amenities. Two swimming pools and cabins fitted with shower, toilet, air-conditioning, telephone and television are just some

of the things that make a stay on board pleasant. Every day, the restaurant serves culinary delights accompanied by exquisite wines.

What stands out is the informal atmosphere. Like almost all other cruise ships, a captain's dinner is also held on the Star Flyer, but nobody appears in a dinner jacket or ball gown. Nor is it expected. This is about real sailing and everything that goes with it.

If you wish, you can help the crew keep the ship on course by sighting the sun with the sextant, standing at the helm or helping to hoist the sails. Don't feel like it? No problem! Then simply take your cocktail of the day and go and laze on a sun beds on one of the three decks and listen to the murmur of the water or the gentle creaking of the teak deck while enjoying the balmy sea breeze.

Compared to a normal cruise ship, this type of holiday is likely to be more energetic on account of the many water sport facilities available on board. You feel like going waterskiing? Then simply tell someone from the sports team and it will be arranged. It is even possible to obtain a PADI diving certificate during the cruise.

The smaller scale of the four-master (180 passengers) makes for a more relaxed atmosphere. You quickly get to know most of the passengers and crew. The captain is always approachable and normally looks in at the bar on the deck in the evening for a coffee and a chat. This is not usually customary on a 'normal' cruise ship.

Mikael Krafft clearly enjoys his ship. As a young boy, the Swedish shipowner lived near the famous Plyms shipyard in Saltsjobaden. There, he listened to stories from carpenters about the romance of the great sailing ships. And when he was given a sailing dinghy on his tenth birthday, there was no going back. Mikael secretly took his boat to visit the Pommern, a windjammer moored in Aland as a museum ship. He climbed on board unnoticed and was moved by the splendour of the vessel. He promised himself that if ever the opportunity arose, he would build a ship like that himself.

Years later, Mikael ended up in the shipbroking business. He took over a small but sound shipping company and built up an empire of transport vessels. The idea of building a tall ship was still in his mind. The costs alone were a problem and Mikael did not have the money needed to design and build a ship. But he came up with the simple and clever idea of building two identical vessels which would be significantly less costly than building one ship. Mikael fulfilled his dream with the creation of the identical twins, the Star Flyer and the Star Clipper.

Montego Bay, 30 March. Today, climbed up the mast after a bet. Another lesson learned: Never make bets during happy hour! Anyway, after two cocktails, I did at least dare to try the big climb. Once in the crow's nest, I realised just how high I was poised above sea level. Really windy, but what a view! The wind in my hair gave me a 'King of the World' feeling. Leonardo Di Caprio, eat your heart out!

Clippers are sailing ships that became popular in the middle of the 19th century, especially because of their speed. Speed became necessary so that slaves from Africa could be transported to the Caribbean in a shorter length of time. The longer the voyage, the more food was needed and there was a greater chance of disease and sickness on board. Another reason for the demand for fast ships was the trade of perishable goods as well as opium and tea from China to Europe and America. Rapid transport was the order of the day. For example, double the price was paid for the first cargo of tea in London compared to the second load.

The best known designer of clippers was the American, Donald McKay, who ran a shipyard in East Boston. His stylish designs (a strikingly long and elegant bow) were very successful. His Flying Cloud from 1851, intended for the transportation of tea, was the fastest clipper of her time and one of the fastest clippers ever built. It was this type of ship that inspired the designers of the Star Flyer to create a similar elegant lady of the sea, and in 1991 it became the first clipper built in over 100 years that could actually sail.

SEADREAM II

PASSENGER/SPACE RATIO   CREW/PASSENGER RATIO

XS   38.7   1.2

Advertising slogans are often far from the truth, or grossly exaggerated. But this is not true of the SeaDream Yacht Club. Because its motto: 'It's yachting, not cruising' hits the nail right on the head.

There are only two ships in operation for the SeaDream Yacht Club. They are identical and are named quite simply SeaDream I and SeaDream II. Yet, anyone cruising on either of these two ships will quickly notice that the service is anything but simple.

The 112 passengers are, indeed, totally pampered by as many as 95 crew members. This passenger-crew ratio is rare in the cruise industry. The small scale of the vessel and the informal atmosphere really does give guests the feeling – just as the slogan promises – of sailing on their own private yacht. The crew quickly learn your name and what favourite drink to pour you during happy hour, lunch and dinner.

St. Tropez, 16 May. Slept late today and didn't go for breakfast on the outer deck until 10 o'clock. Fellow-passenger Ronald also showed late, so we ate together. Right away we made a bet on when we would hear the first 'pop' of a champagne cork. I was the closest with 11 o'clock, he didn't think it would happen until half an hour later. We had just finished eating when Victor came by to ask us if we would like a glass of champers. We said 'yes', of course. And it tasted great... A perfect way to start a day on holiday!

The retractable marina platform at the stern of SeaDream II enhances the 'private yacht' feeling. When possible, the platform is lowered and the fun begins: snorkelling gear, glass-bottom kayaks, laser sailing dinghies, jet skis, paddle boards – everything is ready to go, and at no extra cost since SeaDream II is an all-inclusive ship. The crew ensures everything is safe before taking the guests out on an exciting speedboat trip. Feel like water skiing? Done! Prefer to go on the notorious banana boat with a group of people? No problem. There are also mountain bikes for the guests to use on shore and are useful when exploring hilly areas. Golfers can head to the golf simulator where 30 famous courses can be played. For those interested in culinary pursuits, there is the chance to go shopping at local markets with the chef. These ingredients are then used to prepare a tasty dinner on board.

The Champagne & Caviar Splash during cruises in the Caribbean is a well-known event. The ship drops anchor in a picturesque bay and the passengers are taken to an idyllic beach on a deserted island, where a gourmet barbecue is prepared. But not before some of the crew, standing waist-high in the sea, serve the guests champagne and caviar presented on a surfboard.

Decadent? Sure, but also an original and unforgettable example of luxury living which is all part of the super-yacht experience.

SeaDream offers its guests unique options. For example, what cruise ship gives you the opportunity to spend the night outside under a starry sky? This is possible on the SeaDream ships in the Balinese beds on the top deck. Romantic moments and memories are guaranteed.

Cannes, 17 May. Have just returned from the Top of the Yacht Bar where a bald American in surgical clothing came and stood next to me. Didn't get it. He turned out to be a surgeon using surgical clothing as pyjamas. Strange, since everyone was given a gift of personalised pyjamas at the start of the cruise. Whatever. He and his wife are spending the night under the stars. We had a drink together, then I came back to my cabin to give them some privacy. They were really excited and it's a balmy night, so I think there will be two very happy people walking around the ship tomorrow...

Their modest dimensions enable the SeaDream ships to go to places other ships can't reach: small, picturesque harbours and spectacular bays that are inaccessible for larger vessels. For this reason, SeaDream Yacht Club also offers exclusive cruises through the Amazon region. Yes, that is 'yachting, not cruising'.

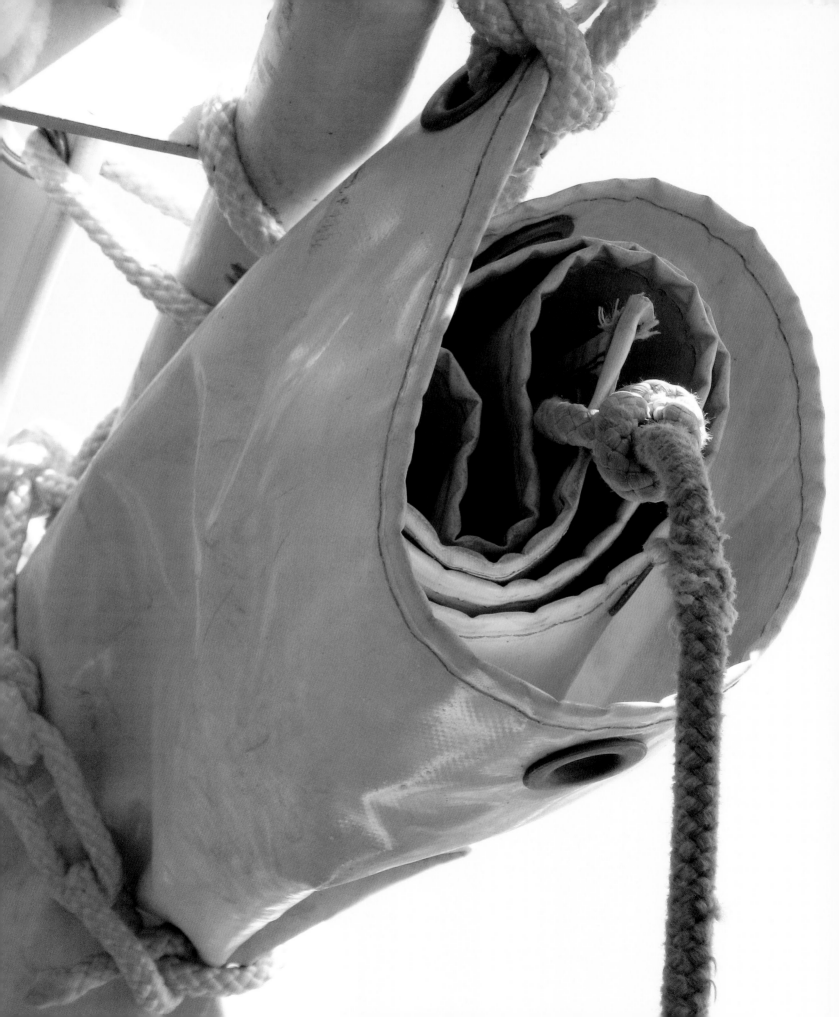

LISBON

The Portuguese capital, Lisbon, has a rich maritime history. In the district of Belém, there is a monument to the national seafarers who embarked on their voyages of discovery across the world from there.

Lisbon, the political, economic and cultural centre of Portugal, is built on the hilly north bank of the Tagus River. The many differences in elevation provide for fantastic views of the surrounding area and especially the river at various locations in the city. Lisbon has almost 3.5 million inhabitants and, including the suburbs, covers an area of around 1,000 sq. kilometres.

Belém lies at the mouth of the Tagus and is now a green area full of museums, restaurants and parks. It was from here that the caravels (fast sailing ships from Portugal and Spain) embarked on their voyages of discovery during Portugal's Golden Age.

The pompous Padrão dos Descobrimentos (Monument to the Discoveries), with the shape of a sword discernible on the front, was erected in 1960 during the Salazar regime on the occasion of the 500th anniversary of the death of Henry the Navigator. He was the first in a long series of Portuguese explorers who procured great wealth for the country.

The 52-metre-high monument features a stylised form of a caravel with billowing sails. Various explorers, scientists, artists and sailors who played an important role at the time are depicted on the ship. Standing prominently at the bow, facing the Tagus, is Henry the Navigator,

holding a model of the type of ship that was so important for the voyages of discovery. He is accompanied by famous men such as Pedro Álvares Cabral (who discovered Brazil), Fernão Magelhães (the most important explorer of his time after Columbus) and Vasco da Gama. Da Gama was very important for Lisbon on account of discovering the route to India by sailing around the Cape of Good Hope. This created a trade route between India and Portugal on which mainly spices were transported. The spice trade made Lisbon the centre of Europe and brought great wealth to the city. In gratitude for this, King Manuel I commissioned the building of the famous Belém Tower and a monastery, Mosteiro dos Jerónimos, which are now well-known attractions in Belém.

Changing exhibitions can be seen at the Monument to the Discoveries. There is an open terrace at the top which can be reached by lift. This provides a magnificent view of the surroundings, including the Belém Tower, the Jerónimos Monastery and the huge marble compass (50 metres in diameter) with the map of the world on the square in front of the monument. This was a gift from South Africa. The routes of the Portuguese explorers from the 15th and 16th centuries can be seen on the map, imaginatively decorated with mermaids, galleons and sea monsters.

ROYAL CLIPPER

The cruise ship with the most charisma is undoubtedly the Royal Clipper under full sail. There is no ship that sails more graciously in international waters. This windjammer may appear ancient, but it was only commissioned in 2000.

The Royal Clipper is the realisation of the childhood dream of Mikael Krafft, owner of the Star Clippers shipping company. As a small boy, he had a photograph of the Preussen hanging above his bed and it was this ship that inspired him to build the Royal Clipper. The Preussen was built in 1902 by the German Tecklenborg shipyard. The unique five-master was known as the fastest sailing ship in the world. She was an impressive 132 metres long and had as many as 47 sails with a total area of 6,806 sq. metres. Windjammers, the class the Preussen belonged to, were used mainly to transport the largest possible quantity of goods in the shortest time possible.

This speed ultimately proved fatal for the Preussen in 1910, when she was rammed by the steamship, the Brighton, off the coast of England during a voyage to South America. The captain of the Brighton later admitted that he had underestimated the speed of the Preussen and assumed that he could quickly pass in front of the sailing ship. Despite the steel hull, the Preussen eventually sank. Fortunately, it was possible to save a large part of the cargo (including pianos destined for Chile) as well as the crew. The accident marked the end of the windjammer era, with steamships taking over the transportation of goods at the beginning of the 20th century.

After Mikael Krafft had finished building the Star Clipper and its twin, the Star Flyer, the time was right to build the ship of his dreams. When the hull of a sailing ship was put up for sale in Poland due to the client's financial difficulties, the Swede took his chance. He had the hull adapted and then towed to the Netherlands, where the ship was completed at the Merwede shipyard.

The Royal Clipper is certainly not a replica of the Preussen (Royal Windjammer would have perhaps been a more applicable name); the design is merely based on the old lady of the sea. And it has been adapted to today's requirements and is equipped with facilities like air-conditioning and Wi-Fi.

The Royal Clipper, 134 metres long, is the largest square-rigged sailing ship in the world. The five masts tower about 60 metres above the surface of the water with a total area of 5,202 sq. metres. Krafft designed the entire sail plan.

The hoisting of the sails is an experience in itself. The bombastic music of Vangelis' '1492, The Conquest of Paradise' blares out over the deck as one sail slowly unfurls after another – 42 times! It is a show that no passenger wants to miss and the sun deck is a hive of activity at moments like this.

A deck that is strewn with ropes, winches, pulleys and everything needed to get and keep a sailing ship of this size going; A sailor sits at a sturdy sewing machine stitching torn sails is a regular sight; A railing gets a new coat of paint. Ship maintenance continues on a daily basis.

Tangier, 1 May. Today, late in the afternoon, left port amid great interest. First, using the engine, then once on the open sea, the show began. Vangelis' dramatic music resounded through the speakers as the sails emerged one by one. I stood admiring the spectacle while enjoying a 'cocktail of the day', a Sea Breeze (how appropriate). When the sails caught the wind, a serene calm descended over the ship. The only sound I could hear was the gentle creaking of the teak deck. A sort of Zen moment.

The interior of the Royal Clipper is just what you would expect from a ship of this calibre: tasteful and decorated with dark wood panelling and lots of gleaming brass. The cabins are comfortable and cosy. No balcony, but some suites do have their own veranda. The red plush sofas and chairs, Art Deco light bulbs and brass fittings give the beautiful Clipper Restaurant on the Commodore deck the aura and allure of a Parisian brasserie. In the evening, the menu here is à la carte, while lunch is served as a buffet with themes such as Italy or Fruit de Mer. Guests can enjoy an elaborate breakfast in the Clipper, while the Piano Bar serves a simple breakfast until late in the morning.

One of the three swimming pools on the sun deck has a glass bottom. This pool is situated above the central staircase, creating light for the Piano Lounge and the lower Clipper Restaurant. The sight of the swimmers floundering about puts a smile on the faces of the guests sitting inside.

Do not expect any Las Vegas-style shows in the evening; a fashion show on the outer deck where the crew present clothes from the boutique is pretty much it. Or, at best, a folk group from the local village give a performance on board. No sun bed service on the sun deck, you simply get the drinks yourself from the Tropical Bar.

3 May, Ibiza. Today, after dinner, went to the outside deck to soak up the atmosphere. It was already dark but the festive lighting created a unique ambiance on board. The temperature was fine, a sweater was quite sufficient. Shared the experiences of the day with some fellow passengers, then looked in at the Tropical Bar. There was something special going on: crew members had put numbers on the backs of a few crabs and got them to run a mini-course over the deck. You could bet on which crab would be the fastest, just like in a horse race. Well, it definitely wasn't going to be my number 3 which looked half asleep. Hilarious to see adult people standing around in a circle ecstatically trying to urge on a few crabs...

Cruising on a tall ship may be special, but sailing on the Royal Clipper has that little bit extra. The atmosphere is relaxed, friendly and informal. You feel part of a large family together with the crew and the other passengers. It really is an amazing feeling to be a guest on the largest sailing ship in the world.

S

SMALL SHIPS

S

If you don't care for mass tourism and find boutique ships too small, then small ships are a good option. The majority of vessels in this book falls into this category. These can typically accommodate between 251 to 750 passengers – perhaps the ideal size for an exclusive cruise. They are agile and small enough to berth at secluded and exclusive destinations, but large enough to offer a full range of on-board entertainment and facilities. This is in contrast to boutique ships which generally offer only very modest evening entertainment programmes, if at all.

Small ships are often big enough to have a theatre on board. Shows can range from acrobatics and classical concerts to real Broadway musicals and plays, as you will find aboard the Seven Seas Voyager. The adage in the cruising world is that the larger the ship the bigger the show, but that of course says nothing about its quality! On some smaller vessels, the level is remarkably high. Another advantage of the smaller venue is that the theatres are intimate, placing the audience much closer to the action. Some small ships offer their guests further excitement by featuring an on-board casino in addition to the usual range of clubs, lounges and bars.

Food is an important part of any holiday, and that also applies to luxury cruises. Think about it: The first thing people are asked when they return home from a holiday is always, 'How was the weather?' followed by, 'Was the food good?' On all cruise ships lots of attention is given to the food. And not just its quality; presentation and variety are equally important aspects.

While the small size of boutique ships leaves room for only a single restaurant, larger ships can offer more dining options. such as the L'Austral and Le Boréal (both with a capacity of 264 passengers) which, in addition to an à la carte restaurant, have a second dining option in the form of an informal self-service restaurant, offering guests the opportunity to breakfast, lunch or dine outdoors on the deck. A slightly larger ship, like the Silver Cloud (296 passengers), has three different restaurants to choose from: a general, a buffet and a specialty restaurant. Larger vessels such as the Nautica have multiple dining options. Eating good food for seven days is no hardship, but variety in the cuisine and surroundings adds extra pleasure to a trip.

Germany's Hapag Lloyd shipping company is very much aware of this. Its newest ship, the Europa 2, carries just 500 passengers yet has eight different restaurants on board including specialty restaurants offering French, Japanese and Asian cuisine, each with a magnificent decor. This means that passengers on a 7-day cruise can enjoy a variety of culinary delights in different setting every night of the week. Now, if that's not luxury...

EUROPA 2

For years, people have been looking forward expectantly to the successor to Hapag Lloyd's Europa, one of the world's highest-rated cruise ships. Finally, in May 2013, the Europa 2 was christened in Hamburg. This beautifully designed vessel exceeds even the highest of expectations.

What immediately strikes you aboard Europa 2 is its size; it is a huge ship for just 500 passengers, offering an unprecedented passenger/space ratio of 85.7. This number is determined by dividing the gross tonnage of the vessel (in this case 42,830 tonnes) by the number of passengers. The higher the number, the more space each passenger has on board.

The design is elegant, modern and German; a little *Porsche meets Audi* with a touch of Bauhaus. Many light wood colours are combined with materials such as stainless steel and silver leaf, the latter used, for example, in the ceiling of the strikingly bright atrium. Both the interior and exterior are designed by Hamburg agency Partner Ship Design whose founders, Siegfried Schindler and Kai Bunge, are both shipbuilding experts and interior designers. This combination enables them to design an entire ship for a ship owner, which is quite unique in the marine industry. The guiding principle in the design of Europa 2 was quality, expressed without resorting to the use of marble, gold taps and the like. Understated quality and workmanship, in line with the *Zeitgeist,* is what both the designers and Hapag Lloyd were aiming for.

According to Schindler, the colours of the interior were inspired by nature, since nature offers harmonic design combinations in which everyone feels comfortable: 'Take a forest in autumn, it's pure harmony.' This explains why earthy tones such as shades of brown, combined with beige and white, are a distinctive feature of Europa 2. And it works: as a guest you quickly feel at home and comfortable on this ship.

The environment was also taken into account in the design process, with various measures taken to minimize CO_2 emissions.

Hapag Lloyd is hoping that Europa 2 will attract a more international clientele, unlike the Europa which is more focused on the German market. The languages spoken on the ship are English and German. Europa 2 cruises are perfect for those looking for a weeklong vacation, or an even shorter four-day excursion. Potential guests are cosmopolitan professionals who have little time for vacations, and when they do take them they want the very best quality.

Such guests can eat in a different restaurant every day at no additional charge because the ship has no fewer than eight restaurants, ranging from the large Weltmeere restaurant and the Tarragon restaurant decorated in French Belle Epoque style, through to the Sushi Sakura restaurant and the Asian Elements restaurant. There are no fixed meal times and every restaurant has plenty of tables for two, which is often lacking on other ships. The dress code is smart casual and there is no Captain's Dinner.

At sea, 6 May. Today we extensively explored the ship. Sometimes it seems as if the ship is only half full, you have so much space here. I'm impressed by the beautiful design, very much to my taste. I found the Herrenzimmer (Gentlemen's Lounge where women are also welcome), to be insanely beautiful with its dark brown leather armchairs. They have a choice of no less than 35 types of gin there, the largest collection at sea. I ordered a gin and tonic with gin from Germany's Black Forest and immediately lit up a good Cuban cigar. A great combination!

The ship consists solely of suites with ocean views and verandas, ranging in size from 28 to 99 sq. metres. Owner's Suites feature bathrooms that look more like mini-spas. A glass wall gives you a majestic view of the sea while bathing in your whirlpool.

The 890 original contemporary artworks on board are of the highest quality. Today's top artists such as Damien Hirst, Gerhard Richter and David Hockney are each represented, with multiple works on show.

Unlike other luxury vessels, the Europa 2 is not an all-in-clusive ship. This is in itself a bit strange, having to pay for your wine or other spirits in one of the six bars, given that the price per guest per night could be called pretty stiff. However, the en-suite minibar carries beer and soft drinks, and is refilled free of charge.

Children are welcome on board (as they are on the Europa too) and there are three children's clubs to keep them entertained and give parents some quality time alone. Special excursions are organized for children and there are also European-trained nannies to care for children from two years and up.

Southampton, 7 May. Today we breakfasted outdoors in the Yacht Club Restaurant. What a feast. 30 kinds of tea to choose from! No teabags, instead blends of loose tea leaves. Choosing the milk was also a challenge, with no less than seven different types to select from. Thankfully, the German staff, all of whom speak perfect English, were very helpful. Excellent service, first-rate staff... and a delicious breakfast!

The two-storey Pool Deck is situated around the saltwater pool that has a retractable roof. There are Balinese beds and regular sunbeds and in the evening the pool deck is converted into a cinema or party space. Entertainment can be found in the Miele cooking school, but you will search in vain for a casino or slot machine. There is an extensive spa and fitness centre on board, covering an area of no less than 1,000 sq. metres. The intimate two-storey, horseshoe-shaped theatre presents shows with an international character designed specifically for Europa 2. Well-known artists make regular guest appearances here or in the Jazz Club. Cruises with a theme, such as golf (with a golf pro on board who joins guests on the golf courses visited) and gourmet food (master classes, wine and olive oil tastings), are offered on a regular basis.

The Europa 2 offers all the ingredients for a relaxing and carefree holiday, for families, too. All this in a superb, contemporary and stylish atmosphere that brings a new standard to the world of ultra-luxury cruising.

NAUTICA

PASSENGER/SPACE RATIO   CREW/PASSENGER RATIO

S   44.2   1.8

The Nautica is one of the ships from the legacy of the former Renaissance Cruises. The rich decor in British Country Club style is both comfortable and timeless.

In 2001, the US line Renaissance Cruises went bankrupt as a direct result of the attacks on the Twin Towers. Americans were afraid to fly, and Renaissance, already under financial pressure and very vulnerable with eight ships across the world, was directly impacted. As both friend and foe agreed, the problem was certainly not the product.

The eight identical vessels, named rather unimaginatively, R1 to R8, were eventually sold to different cruise lines. Today, the Azamara Club Cruises fleet consists entirely of the former Renaissance ships R6 (now Azamara Journey) and R7 (Azamara Quest). The R3 and R4 now sail as the Pacific Princess and Ocean Princess, while R8, after mixed fortunes, ended up in 2011 with P&O under the new name of Adonia.

Oceania Cruises, established in 2002, also began its life with the purchase of former Renaissance vessels. The R2 was purchased and renamed Regatta, and a year later, in response to the company's growing success, was followed by the purchase of the Insignia (R1). Finally, the R5 was incorporated into the fleet in 2005 and christened Nautica. Recently, the newly-designed and larger Marina and Riviera were also added to the Oceania fleet.

The original Renaissance ships were designed by the Scottish interior architect, John McNeece. He was commissioned to design the entire interior of the ships, which was unusual as it is normal practice for a team of designers to work on different parts of a vessel. The advantage of the single-designer method is that the entire ship exudes the same atmosphere. McNeece drew much of his inspiration from British country clubs, and you quickly sense this.

Aboard the Nautica you will find Chesterfield sofas, thick dark red carpeting, heavy curtains, wood panelling and marble fireplaces with (imitation) open fireplaces. In keeping with the British country club style, you can even find trompe-l'oeil ceiling paintings in the lounge, restaurant and library.

This may make the interior look a little 'heavy', but it creates an undeniable homey ambiance. The entrance is a true eye-catcher with its monumental staircase and (again) richly-decorated banisters. The hallways at the foot of the first and second floor staircases are furnished with expansive, comfortable, seating areas. Thick carpets and numerous softly lit table lamps predominate and the furniture oozes with charm.

In spring 2014, Oceania refurbished the Nautica, Regatta and Insignia. All the cabins were refitted, along with some of the public areas, and given its popularity on the Marina and Riviera, a Barista coffee bar was also added to the Nautica.

Amsterdam, 13 June. Today, we are back on board the Nautica. I've been looking forward to this reunion with the ship that I knew back in its day as a Renaissance vessel. It must be almost 12 years ago that I went on my first cruise to Tahiti. Back then the bow was dark blue, now it is bright white. The weather was also a bit different! It's striking how much on board has remained the same, and although the décor is not entirely to my taste, I still think it's a classy ship where I feel at home.

The size (accommodates 680 passengers and 370 crew) and design of the Nautica make it very easy to find your way around. Moreover, it is small enough to berth in ports where larger ships cannot, but large enough to accommodate a good range of facilities. One example is the Horizon Lounge, which serves as an observation lounge. Location on the top deck, its floor-to-ceiling windows make it an ideal place to relax while sailing. Every day, just before 16:00, a large number of guests congregate here for afternoon tea. Trolleys are rolled in, offering a wide selection of teas, a variety of cakes, petit fours, scones, sandwiches and other delicacies. A live string orchestra softly plays classical chamber music and, yes, here it comes again: that special *lazy Sunday afternoon* feeling...

MUSCAT

Anyone cruising in the Middle East will most likely berth at Muscat as well as Dubai. Yet there could not be a greater contrast between these two cities.

Dubai is a dazzling, ostentatious city with tall skyscrapers and luxurious shopping malls. Muscat is the opposite. The architecture in the modern city is modest and understated, with white houses that set the tone. What does impress, however, is the Sultan Qaboos Grand Mosque – not because of any gaudy showiness, but because of its tasteful design and decoration.

Muscat is the capital of the Sultanate of Oman, most of which consists of desert (82%). Oman is a rich country thanks to the presence of huge oil fields. Under the leadership of Sultan Qaboos bin Said Al Said, who in 1970 deposed his conservative father, the country has developed in recent decades into a modern country, but without denying its traditions. Omanis often spend their free time in the desert where their forefathers dwelled as nomads.

One of the most popular leisure activities in the desert is 'dune bashing', racing four-wheel vehicles through the sand. Air is let out of the four-wheel drive tyres (usually a Toyota Land Cruiser, second only to the camel as the 'King of the Desert') for more grip, and the fun begins. Drivers guide their vehicles as fast as possible over the sand dunes. It's a lot of fun, but not too good for the environment.

Cruise ship passengers can also experience the desert. The huge expanse of sand starts just a three hours drive from Muscat port. Most of the desert tours from the cruise ship are to experience dune bashing or to visit a Bedouin family. When the ship spends several days in Muscat, there is often an opportunity to spend a night in the desert in traditional campsites which offer every luxury. The experience is definitely worth the effort. At night the clear skies are filled with stars and the silence is overwhelming.

With a bit of luck, vacationers in Muscat can also become familiar with another natural phenomenon that is enjoyed by Omanis, namely the wadi – a watery oasis in a dry rocky area, and a complete contrast to the surrounding desert. Whole families gather here to swim, picnic and enjoy nature.

WIND SURF

For the real sailors among us, the Wind Surf is probably not the 'real McCoy'. However, this cruise ship with sails has undeniable charm, even if experts will tell you that it's not a 'real' sailing ship.

If the sails do have to be unfurled, this can be done by the simple push of a button from the ship's bridge. Then they automatically emerge, with no manual work involved. For true sail fanatics this is an abomination, but the Wind Surf's passengers simply shrug their shoulders. This is because the sails create a romantic atmosphere aboard a vessel that is actually an amalgamation of a luxury mega yacht with a modern sailing ship.

The Wind Surf, which made its maiden voyage in 1990 as Club Med I, has gathered a sizeable crowd of faithful fans. A twin ship sails under the name Club Med II for Club Med Cruises, serving mainly the French market, unlike the Wind Surf which targets an international clientele.

With its capacity of 310 passengers the Wind Surf is significantly larger than its smaller siblings, the Wind Star and the Wind Spirit, two identical vessels, each offering room for 148 passengers. The style on board, as it always has been on sailing ships, is informal and gentlemen can leave their jackets and ties at home. Food is important aboard the Wind Surf, with quality and presentation at a high level. The Amphora restaurant serves food that can best be described as California-style nouvelle cuisine. Seating up to 272 guests, it is the largest restaurant on board. Additionally, guests can

opt for the Stella Bistro (124 seats) where food with a French twist is served, while at night the Candles steak restaurant serves open-air dinners around the pool. The Veranda and The Yacht Club are the breakfast and lunch locations. 24-hour room service is also available.

Many water sports can be enjoyed from the folding platform at the back of the ship. Kayaking, waterskiing and windsurfing are all available and included in the price. The fitness centre, on the top Star Desk, with its all-round windows, offers a splendid view to accompany your workout.

The decorative sails give the Wind Surf a romantic look, but they are not just there for show. The five huge masts, the largest 67 metres high, are equipped with a total of seven sails with a total surface area of 2,600 sq. metres, certainly enough to move the cruise ship silently forward. On-board computers ensure that the vessel tilts no more than 6 degrees during the voyage.

Part sailing ship, part mega-yacht, the Wind Surf represents a special phenomenon in the cruise industry, guaranteeing a unique and successful cruise.

LE BORÉAL

Some 25 years ago, four friends from the French naval school were sitting together one evening talking about their futures. They were all agreed on one thing: with too little work around, job prospects did not look good. So why not take matters into their own hands and start a cruise line?

The four friends went looking for investors, who were easily found due to the attractive tax advantages in investing in a cruise line. So it was not long before the three-masted sailing ship Le Ponant was commissioned from a French shipyard et voilà, La Compagnie du Ponant was born. The 32-cabin Le Ponant is still part of the fleet, which now consists of four vessels.

The other three ships are identical, at least from the outside. L'Austral (which means south wind) and Le Boréal (north wind) look like twin sisters, while Le Soléal, which came into service in summer 2013, looks different owing to its lighter coloured hull.

The three sister ships (each with 132 cabins and suites) have a stunning contemporary design, more like contemporary yachts. The Compagnie du Ponant also refers to its ships as mega-yachts.

Walking from the gangplank to the lobby of Le Boréal, one is immediately entranced by the modern artwork prominently displayed. What look like water droplets coming from the ceiling, on closer inspection are actually sharpened plastic stones. The wind turns the stones slowly around their axis to give a sparkling effect.

This two-storey-high 'crystal rain', designed by Giovanna Dessi, is also featured on L'Austral (but not on Le Soléal). The red circular bench around the crystal rain is the very incarnation of a modern and refined interior piece, designed by French architect Jean-Philippe Nuel.

This architect, well-known for his numerous modern hotel interiors, has taken care to ensure his same trademark style is seen throughout the ship. The main colours are white, red and grey. On L'Austral, they are cream, warm grey and caramel, while the interior of Le Soléal is finished in dark brown wood tones, cream and sea green.

It's a smart move by Nuel to give every ship its own identity by means of a colour combination. Le Boréal, with its fresh red accents, gains an especially strong identity of its own. The architect's refinement is evident also from the old black-and-white Côte d'Azur posters, each of which has been given a very subtle red accent.

Life aboard Le Boréal is very pleasant. Cabins are well laid-out, with various smart additions such as the glass wall in the bathroom that allows you to shower with a view over the sea. If, however, you would prefer more privacy during your shower ritual, a sliding panel conceals you from your travel companion. The furnishings are beautiful and contemporary; hip details such as leather handles (like those of an old suitcase) on leather-covered cupboard doors and drawers remind you that you are a guest on a trendy ship. Such coolness is also a reference to the French luxury cruise liners of yesteryear.

Lisbon, 25 April. What a splendid day today. The relaxed atmosphere on board suits me fine. I almost feel like I'm holidaying on my own private yacht. And lunch at Le Commodore was excellent again. I have to be careful with the wine, every time I look the other way, the sommelier Harris tops up my glass again. I think I saw him move away with a smile on his lips. At lunch I normally never drink wine. Well, when in Rome... And it helps with my afternoon nap.

There are two dining options on board, a self-service restaurant on Deck 6 and Le Commodore, the à la carte restaurant on Deck 2. At lunch and dinner, the wine is included and in accordance with French tradition is generously poured. On Deck 6 at the front of the ship there is an intimate panoramic lounge, and a larger lounge (with great coffee!) with a covered outdoor terrace is located at the rear of Deck 3. The only downside is that the view is blocked somewhat by the closed metal railing – the same problem you will encounter on the balcony of your cabin. The reason for this design is that this ship travels to both the North and the South Poles, and the railings are a requirement for sailing in ice-strewn waters.

Le Boréal is a unique ship offering luxury, modern design and intimacy. Its compactness also allows it to berth in remote places where larger ships are unable to dock. The atmosphere on board is laidback and relaxed, thanks also to the friendly bilingual staff, and you quickly feel like you are on your own private yacht — a wonderful feeling.

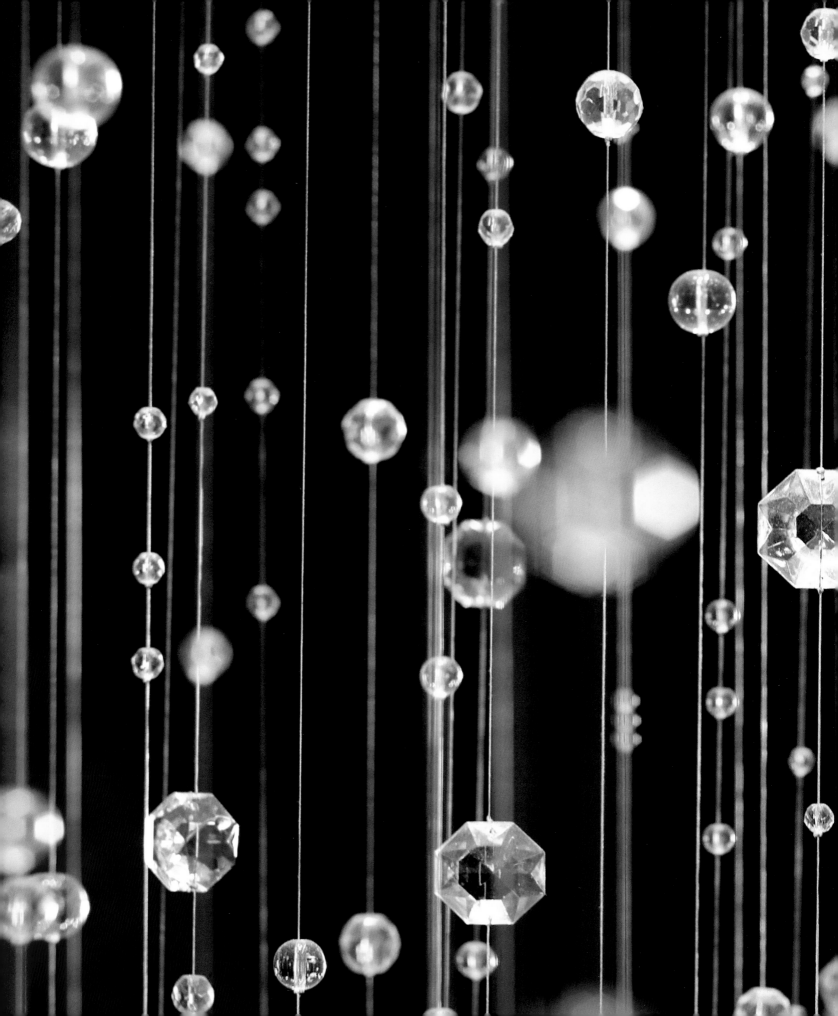

MONACO

One of the most popular destinations for a Mediterranean cruise is Monaco. During a walk around the marina, you quickly learn a lot in a short time about this principality.

The lucky ones can gape from the cruise ship at the many yachts, sailboats and speedboats moored here. The sight of all this beauty, with a variety of tower blocks in the background, is impressive. The striking number of high-rise buildings is for a reason. Building land here is scarce and extremely expensive. Monaco covers an area of just two square kilometres making it, after the Vatican, the smallest independent country in the world. It is very popular with the wealthy, not only because of its natural beauty, but also because Monaco's inhabitants, with the exception of French nationals, do not pay income tax. The city-state has a population of 30,000 inhabitants and is, after Macao, the most densely populated country in the world. Only a small proportion of the population (a mere 17%) are original inhabitants, the so-called Monegasques. The vast majority is French or Italian.

Popular with the rich and famous is the classic Monte Carlo casino and the annual Formula One Grand Prix which has been held in Monaco since 1929, attracting thousands of visitors each year.

A morning walk around the port of the cosmopolitan resort is an experience, with plenty to see. On the moored yachts and ships the day begins with scrubbing the deck, lots of coffee-drinking or a late breakfast. With his back to the water stands the bust of local legend, Louis Chiron, who in the 1950s caused a frenzy as a Formula One driver. In 1950, he made history by finishing third in the Monaco Grand Prix. Chiron's gaze is directed towards the Grimaldi Palace high up on the mountain. This dynasty has ruled here since 1297. A little further down the quay, a mechanic is inspecting the underside of a Riva boat, with another five streamlined boats waiting their turn at the Riva service station. On the other side, the bigger yachts are moored tightly, aft towards the quay. The colourful flags (of offshore tax havens) flutter gaily in the wind. Here people sit chatting on the rear deck, staying cool in the shade.

Clearly, if you have money, Monaco is a great place to live.

L'AUSTRAL

From the outside, L'Austral looks just like her twin sister ship, Le Boréal, yet inside, its colour scheme creates a completely different atmosphere.

Anyone who has been on both Le Boréal and L'Austral will agree that outwardly they look identical, but once aboard, they each have their own unique ambiance. Interior architect Jean-Philippe Nuel has deliberately used different colour palettes to give each vessel its own identity. Otherwise the layout and comfort are the same. Le Boréal comes across as fresh and modern with white, red and light grey tones, while L'Austral is warmer and more traditional, with its combination of caramel, cream and warm grey.

3 July, Korcula. Tonight was the Captain's cocktail party. Luckily the weather was fine so it could be held outside around the pool. The champagne flowed and the Captain introduced the entire crew in gala uniform. Very stylish. Then the party turned into the Captain's dinner with festively laid tables and extra nice bottles of wine were uncorked for the occasion. What a night! Unfortunately, after two days, Venice, our final destination, is already in sight. Have absolutely no desire to go ashore...

There are few cruises where the Captain stands at the bottom of the gangway to introduce himself and personally welcome the guests aboard. This happens on the L'Austral and reinforces the family atmosphere. A cruise on this ship is a bit like sailing on your own private yacht... without the price tag. An excellent option.

SEABOURN SOJOURN

Seabourn is rightfully proud of the many awards it has won and continues to win year after year. Anyone who has experienced the service aboard the Seabourn Sojourn understands this ship's popularity.

The Seabourn Sojourn accommodates 450 passengers. A crew of 330 stands ready to serve and pamper them. Service is what the Seabourn is all about.

With its striking silhouette, the Seabourn Sojourn is recognizable at a single glance, as are its sister ships, the Seabourn Odyssey and the Seabourn Quest. The exterior design is by Yran & Storbraaten, one of the best known architectural firms in the cruise industry. This Norwegian firm also designed most of the interior. While less spectacular than the outside, if anything rather subdued, it remains tasteful and fully-equipped. Scandinavian design is characterized by light wood combined with warm colours such as the wine red carpeting of the central spiral staircase, or the brightly coloured seats in The Restaurant. This restaurant, which can accommodate all the guests in one sitting, features a modern elegant design. Its centrepiece, graceful draperies and an impressive chandelier, gives The Restaurant a sense of spaciousness. The much smaller The Restaurant 2 (50 guests), with its low ceiling, offers a more intimate venue. A third restaurant, the informal The Colonnade, has a terrace. The Patio Grill next to the central pool (Seabourn Sojourn has two swimming pools and six whirlpools) completes the dining options.

Despite its size, the ship retains the atmosphere and feel of a mega-yacht, while still making you feel at home. A nice touch is the central Seabourn Square which houses the concierge, a library, a selection of shops, a coffee shop and a computer centre with Internet facilities. This is a relaxing lounge area with an adjoining terrace where you can enjoy a good book and a cappuccino expertly made by the barista.

As on the sister ships, a whopping 1,098 sq. metres spread over two floors is reserved for health and well-ness facilities. The Spa at Seabourn, in the aft of the ship, is managed by the spa company Elemis.

For those who like privacy there is the ultimate luxury of the Spa Villa, a secluded covered area on the Spa Deck that can be hired exclusively. Here you can enjoy customized spa treatments in the open air. There is a spacious bath, a Balinese bed and a sitting area for lounging and luxurious relaxation. Healthy nibbles and beverages are also served.

On the general-access outside decks guests are regularly treated to a so-called Massage Moment. Wandering masseuses offer spontaneous free neck and shoulder massages to those who want it. And who doesn't?

For sports enthusiasts, the extensive fitness centre and The Marina are pleasant options. Guests can take part in various water sports such as sailing, windsurfing and kayaking from the extendable rear deck.

Amsterdam, 13 June. Enjoyed lunch at The Colonnade on the aft deck. I cannot remember ever tasting such a delicious piece of salmon. The white wine the waiter recommended was good, but only really showed its finesse when complementing the salmon. Perfect combination! It's nice when you can rely on the waiters' knowledge. From now on I shall take their advice without question...

DUBROVNIK

In the south of the Croatian region of Dalmatia is the completely walled city of Dubrovnik, also known as the Pearl of the Adriatic. A walk along the city walls is more than worth it.

You will be rewarded with fantastic views of both the old town and the surrounding area. From one vantage point you look across a sea of red roofs, from another over the Stradun, the main street of the city. A little further on you can stand face to face with the dome of the Velika Gospa cathedral or enjoy a magnificent view of the crystal clear sea.

Dubrovnik was founded in the 7th century, and was originally called Ragusa. Through the centuries it developed as a free city-state and a successful trading point. At its peak in the 15th and 16th centuries Dubrovnik's sea power rivalled that of Venice and the threat of a hostile attack increased. Drastic measures were needed and the existing walls were extended to almost two kilometres in length and up to six metres in width. To make the city a truly impregnable fortress, the walls were further reinforced by adding towers, bastions and other defences. Finally, more than 120 guns completed the fortifications of Dubrovnik.

Its excellent location, high on a cliff, made an attack from the sea unlikely. The walls on that side are therefore quite low. From the landward side the threat of attack was far greater and in some places the walls are 25 metres high! Ultimately, no hostile army dared to attack the city. But an attack came from nature itself: in 1667 an earthquake destroyed large parts of the city.

Anyone visiting Dubrovnik's historic old town, through it's port protected for centuries by the massive St. John's Fort, will be impressed by its beauty. Cathedrals, churches, palaces, marble streets, fountains, each part is as beautiful as the next. Add to this the many cafés and shops and you have a fantastic destination. Since 1979 the old town has been on the Unesco World Heritage List. While half of the centre was damaged in 1991 during the civil war, it has, since then, fortunately been restored to its former glory.

poivrer l'échalote ... des-
...nd de beurre ... la
... Cuire ... sur
feu modéré ... 1/4 h
arroser en c... ...on
... pas dess... Dresser
... Servir très chaud. Daurade
...es et aux épices 4 daurades
...poivron vert, 1 poivron rouge,
1/2 cuillère à café de curry,
...café de cumin, 1/2 cuillère
...curcuma, sel, piment de-
...cayenne,

moitié d...
saler et p...
badigeonn...
fleur de thy...
un grill à p...
environ. ...
(surtout n...
... su...
aux aroma...
de 500g, 1 p...
2 tomates, 1...
1/2 cuillère à...
à café de c...
cayenne, 2...

SEVEN SEAS VOYAGER

PASSENGER/SPACE RATIO   CREW/PASSENGER RATIO

S   59.8   1.6

Some ships give you that home-away-from-home feeling the moment you step aboard. The ultra-luxurious Seven Seas Voyager is such a ship.

The first thing that strikes you aboard the Voyager is the sensation of space. It's a matter of taste, of course, but the interior of the ship is so crisp, bright and well laid-out that in no time at all you will find your way around and feel at home. The ship is a medium-sized vessel of about 42,000 tons. With 700 passengers, that gives it a high passenger/space ratio.

The central staircase (there are three in total) is open, making it easy to find one's way around. The interior has a Scandinavian feel to it, with light wood everywhere. The hallways are wide, and all suites look outward, so the ship has a simple layout: the cabin deck has a central corridor with suites to the left and the right. The layout is equally simple on the other decks.

A lot of space aboard the Seven Seas Voyager is devoted to its various restaurants. The Compass Rose restaurant is the largest, with 570 seats. You can also opt for the trendy French specialty restaurant Signatures (120 seats) where you can enjoy foie gras and frog legs. The kitchen here is run by chefs trained at the prestigious Le Cordon Bleu. The American-style Prime Steakhouse 7 is for the true carnivore and with a seating capacity of 80, is the ship's smallest restaurant. The informal self-service La Veranda restaurant with both indoor and outdoor seating for 450 passengers completes the range. As always, there is no additional charge for eating in one of the specialty restaurants.

Amsterdam, 13 June. Lunched today in Compass Rose. What a nice, balanced meal. The pumpkin soup as a starter was velvety smooth and the lobster appetizer was delicious, but the main course beat everything. That tournedos was so tasty and tender. They tell me the meat comes from Colorado because they can deliver top quality. Well, hooray for Colorado Cows! The Sicilian red wine with it was perfect, bringing out the flavour of the meat. I'm not a dessert person, but I couldn't refuse the chocolate dessert. It proved a wonderful end to a perfect lunch. This is quality you will only be served in the best restaurants on land. I observe that I am eating rather more than usual. Anyway, will be exploring the city tomorrow on foot...

With the introduction of the Seven Seas Mariner and Seven Seas Voyager, Regent Seven Seas Cruises was the first cruise company to introduce suite-only ships, and all with balconies. The fleet also includes the smaller Seven Seas Navigator (490 passengers), also suites-only, and 90% of these have a balcony. Recently all three ships underwent major refurbishing at a cost of 40 million dollars.

It's great to have space aboard a cruise ship, but it is the service which makes all the difference. The Voyager's crew of 445 do everything to please their passengers. In addition, this is a truly all-inclusive ship because food, drink, and excursions are included in the cruise price. Passengers can even go on several excursions a day at no additional cost. Thanks to all this, the Seven Seas Voyager can truly call itself an ultra-luxury cruise ship.

SILVER CLOUD

The Silver Cloud, the first ship of Silversea Cruises, founded by the Italian Lefebvre family in 1994, continues to ply the seas to everyone's satisfaction.

Virginal white on the outside and warm tones inside, the interior of the Silver Cloud underwent a total makeover in 2012, bringing it up to its current standard. Not a modern interior, on the contrary, but that's not what Silversea's generally older clientele comes looking for. The ship's Art Deco influence is particularly noticeable in Le Champagne, the only floating restaurant run by Relais & Chateau. Its dark wood wall panels inlaid with brass stripes, the chairs and lighting all breathe Art Deco. The ship's staircase, the armchairs in The Bar, the ornate ceiling in The Restaurant and the entrance doors to the Italian La Terrazza restaurant hark back to 1930s style. Silversea has very consciously added these style elements as a subtle nod to what, in their eyes, was the golden age of cruising.

The 296 guests sailing with the Silver Cloud will want for nothing: the 222-strong crew will make sure of that.

The food on offer, often with an Italian twist, is of high quality. The central The Restaurant is a somewhat dark but elegantly-furnished venue. Christofle silver cutlery and Eschenbach porcelain adorn the tables. Silversea applies the all-inclusive principle and for this reason selected wines during lunch and dinner are available in all three restaurants at no additional cost. For real wine buffs there is an extensive 'connoisseur's list' with a selection of superior wines which are paid for separately.

The restaurants operate an 'open seating' dinner policy, with guests deciding where and with whom they eat.

The 148 suites (all Silversea ships have only guest accommodation with separate living areas) all have sea views, butler service and are classically furnished. Nowhere is the interior loud or extravagant. Most of the suites feature a teak veranda.

What makes the stay on board so pleasant is the space and tranquillity you have as a passenger. You will not run up against long queues of people waiting for a buffet lunch at La Terrazza. There are no loudspeaker announcements. Nor do you sign chits for drinks, as everything (liquor, cocktails and champagne) is included. Only excursions and spa treatments require additional payment. The Silversea service is legendary, and not just on board. At most ports of call, shuttle buses stand ready to take guests to the city centre and pick them up again, all free of charge. It is these little extras that make life aboard the Silver Cloud very pleasant. The ship is perfect for people who value good conversation, enjoy good food and drink, and who like to dress nicely for dinner. With an average of two 'formal nights' during a cruise of seven days, the atmosphere is somewhat more formal, and the staff wear white tie.

There is entertainment in The Show Lounge and there is a casino on board, but most guests come here to find peace and quiet and be pampered by highly-trained personnel ready to satisfy their every whim.

Silversea is one of the few luxury cruise lines that is small and intimate. The largest vessel of the seven-ship fleet, the Silver Spirit, can accommodate 540 passengers. The latest addition, the Silver Galapagos, is a boutique ship with room for just 100 guests. This expedition ship sails in the region from which it takes its name, and where Darwin developed his Theory of Evolution. The other expedition ship in the fleet, the Silver Explorer accommodates 132 passengers and sails to both the North and South Poles.

What makes Silversea unique is that its guests, provided they book a minimum five-night cruise, can start and end their journey where they wish. These customized cruises demonstrate once again what Silversea is all about: its guests.

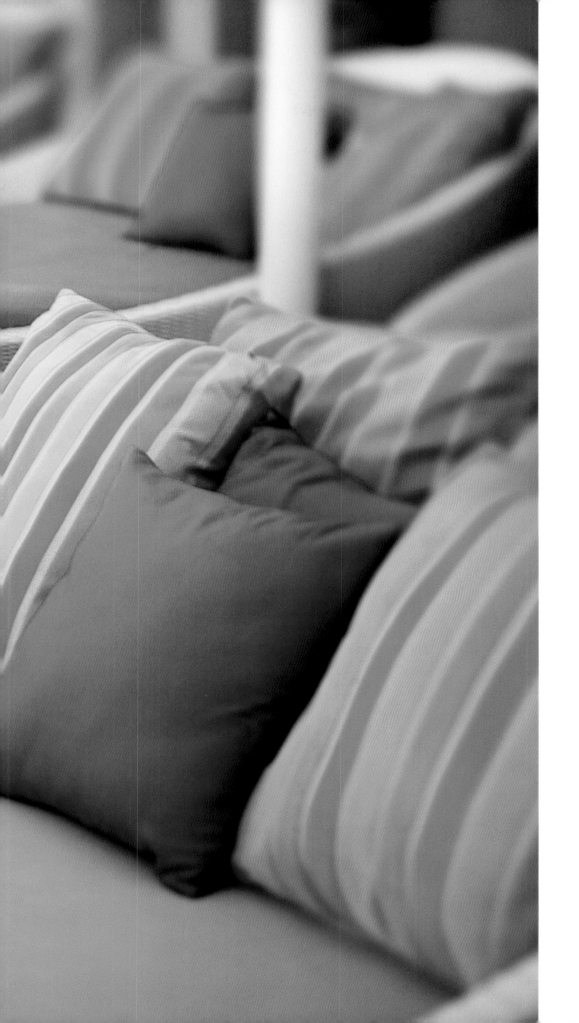

M

MID-SIZED SHIPS

Mid-sized ships are vessels that can carry between 751 and 1750 passengers. The advantage that they offer is that there is more entertainment on board – theatres, cinemas, bars, lounges, lectures and workshops – compared to a boutique or small ship.

You can also live more anonymously if you are someone who likes your privacy. Naturally, the opposite is also true: The more people there are on board, the greater the chance of you meeting someone you click with and can hang out with during the cruise. Indeed, lifelong friendships often start on a cruise ship.

For those travelling alone (and that's an average of 1 in 4 people), it is a good idea to indicate in advance where you would like to sit for dinner. Eating alone is an option, of course. Those who would like to meet fellow passengers can choose to be seated at a table for six, eight or ten persons.

As there are generally more (older) women on a cruise than men, Cunard introduced in the mid 1970's what are known as 'gentlemen hosts' on board the Queen Elizabeth 2. These gentlemen, young retirees with proven dancing skills, are not just dance partners for single ladies, they also provide company (if wished) during excursions, cocktail parties or dinner. This concept of gentlemen hosts proved so successful that it was also adopted by cruise operators such as Crystal Cruises, Holland America Line, Silversea and Regent Seven Seas Cruises.

Those who do not want to go on a cruise but would simply like to spend the night on a cruise ship can do this in Rotterdam. This is where the former flagship of the Holland America Line, the SS Rotterdam, is moored at the quay. Having retired from cruising, the former ocean liner now serves as a hotel, entertainment and congress centre. This is a tried and tested concept. For example, the Queen Mary, former pride of the Cunard Line, has been at the quayside in Long Beach (California) since 1967 after operating as an ocean liner for 31 years. She now also serves as a hotel and congress centre.

Following a refit and refurbishment lasting several years, the SS Rotterdam has more or less been restored to her original state. The furniture has been re-upholstered and works of art restored. The ship now acts as a kind of time machine, taking people back to the 1950's. The exterior stands out with its graceful stern and elegant bow, designed to subdue the highest waves of the Atlantic Ocean. This makes its silhouette much more beautiful and distinguished than that of most modern cruise ships.

In order to create hotel rooms that meet today's requirements and expectations, two cabins were converted into one. This says a lot about the level of comfort on board the cruise ships in those days.

RIVIERA

When Oceania Cruises ordered two new ships a few years ago, the company had a clear goal in mind: to build the most elegant five-star cruise ships of the time. This goal was achieved with the creation of the (almost) identical Marina and Riviera.

The sparkling white, streamlined Riviera flaunts herself in the sun. The 16-deck ship has space for 1,250 passengers and around 800 staff. Oddly enough, though, you don't feel you are on board with more than 2,000 people because there is so much space for each passenger. This makes the Riviera feel like a much smaller and more intimate ship.

Oceania attaches great importance to serving delicious food and drinks. A large space is devoted to the galley (though professional kitchen would be a more appropriate term). So large, in fact, that while the Riviera was being built at the Fincantieri shipyard in Italy, there was a joke among the workers that they weren't building a cruise ship, but a floating galley. From this galley, the cooks have to serve as many as six restaurants.

The most eye-catching of these is the Grand Dining Room, which seats 566 guests. This restaurant is located on the afterdeck of deck six and has many windows. The rear of the restaurant is made almost entirely of glass so that the room is bathed in light during the day. At night, the lighting is provided by the huge crystal Swarovski chandelier, an absolutely magnificent piece. The tasteful combination of dark wood panelling, cognac-coloured chairs, carpeting and a selection of modern art (with a lot of sculptures)

makes it an extremely pleasant room to dine in. This feeling is further enhanced by fine linen, Riedel glassware, Versace porcelain and Christofle silver cutlery.

The intimate Italian Toscana restaurant, the Polo Grill (traditional American steakhouse), the French Jacques (named after head chef Jacques Pepin, Oceania's culinary adviser and a former chef for President De Gaulle) and Red Ginger (Asian fusion cuisine) are popular speciality restaurants for which reservations have to be made. La Réserve, Privée, Waves and the self-service Terrace Café (with a lovely terrace on the aft deck) complete the variety of fine-dining options. Due to its exceptional high quality of food, Oceania has become known as the 'foodie cruise line'.

The atmosphere, described as 'Country Club Casual', is informal and relaxed. This means that there are no Captain's dinners.

Livorno, 21 October. Today, I celebrated my birthday in the Red Ginger, and had the restaurant's signature dish, sea bass steamed in banana leaves. Rarely tasted anything that delicious! For desert, they gave me a cake with 'Happy Birthday, Iwein' iced on it. Really thoughtful. It took quite some effort to get the staff to stop singing to me. All in all, an unforgettable evening.

The interior was designed by the Norwegian interior designers and architects, Petter Yran and Bjorn Storbraaten, the founders of Y&S Architects in Oslo and very well known in the cruise industry. The three Owner's Suites are the ship's showpieces, fitted out with furniture and accessories from the Ralph Lauren Home collection. Located on the aft deck, these suites each cover a very generous area of 186 sq. metres. Among other things, they have their own private fitness room, a Jacuzzi on the balcony and a Yamaha baby grand piano for musical guests.

The use of expensive and tasteful materials gives the ship a distinguished look, comparable to top hotels on the mainland. Take the lobby, for example, with the eye-catching Grand Staircase styled in the shape of a horseshoe.

This staircase, decorated with crystal medallions and columns, was designed by the French company, Lalique, a name that was famous in the Art Deco period for spectacular jewellery and crystal designs. A total of 37 artists took 1,600 hours to hand craft the 2,100 kilograms of crystal. The table and vase are also made of crystal.

Throughout the entire ship, visitors can marvel at an art collection worth millions of dollars. The CEO of Oceania, Frank Del Rio, is an avid art collector. Together with Vice-Chairman Bob Binder, he roamed auctions and galleries selecting more than 1,000 works of art to adorn the Riviera. The objective was to bring together a prestigious collection of modern art unparalleled on cruise ships. It was important for Del Rio to choose works of art that would prompt discussion and encourage contemplation.

So he did not shy away from controversial works. Del Rio's background (he was born in Cuba but fled to America at the age of seven with his parents) means that guests can admire a large number of works by Latin-American artists, such as the Cuban Vanguard Movement that caused quite a stir from 1927 to 1950. Contemporary Cuban artists like Julio Larraz and José Grillo are also represented.

All in all, the discerning traveller will not be bored for one moment on this elegant, stylish five-star cruise ship. The beautiful interior is consciously kept timeless so as to continue attracting plenty of passengers in the future. Elegance, luxury and good taste simply never go out of fashion.

MS ROTTERDAM

When NASM was established in 1873, the shipping company's first steamship was given the name of its home base, Rotterdam. More than 140 years later, the name was changed to Holland America Line, but the company once again has a ship called Rotterdam in its fleet.

It took a long time for the Netherlands-American Steamship Company (in short NASM) to see the light of day. But once it did, things worked out very well. In 1875, the New Waterway was opened, making Rotterdam a major port. It was the time when many Europeans, often with the entire contents of their homes, emigrated to America to try their luck there. A regular service was therefore established between the Dutch city and New York, which turned out to be very profitable.

The Rotterdam-New York route was colloquially known as the 'Holland-America Line' and in 1896 this name was added to the official company name. The abbreviation HAL eventually became a household name.

With the emergence of air travel, the transatlantic crossing became less profitable, causing HAL to focus increasingly on the cruise business. In 1971, it operated its very last transatlantic crossing on the ship New Amsterdam. In 1989, the company, now called Holland America Line, was taken over by the American concern, Carnival Cruise Lines, which it is still part of.

The original home base has regularly been honoured over the years, and the MS Rotterdam is the sixth ship to receive this name, sometimes denoted by the addition of the Roman numeral VI or 6.

It is a ship of the so-called R class, to which the Volendam (1999) as well as the Amsterdam and the Zaandam (both from 2000) belong. All of the ships operated by NASM and Holland America Line are named after a Dutch place that ends in 'dam', although some names are imaginary (such as Eurodam).

A distinctive feature of the layout of the R class vessels is their light-hearted design. Or, as the ship's interior designer from studio VFD, architect Frans Dingemans, puts it: 'In naval architecture, the art is to provide diversity and variation while maintaining peace and quiet and safety. Ships tend to be boring and symmetrical. It is so simple to cram all the engineering into the centre and arrange the cabins and other areas around this. But my ships are not symmetrical. They have passageways that twist and wind their way through the interior like forest trails.'

This means that walking through the ship initially feels like a tour of discovery, with a new surprise looming at every turn. Dingemans' input is clearly visible in the spectacular atrium, located on the port side instead of in the centre, as is normal on cruise ships.

Rotterdam, 11 December. Took a bit of getting used to today on board the ship, but now I do see the logic of the layout. It's remarkable how many alcoves and corners there are where you can sit and relax on the most colourful and comfortable seats and armchairs. Wandering through the ship led from one surprise to another. Near the library there were even life-size replicas of soldiers from the famous Chinese Terracotta Army! This ship feels like a cosy second home...

Dutch history is very much a part of the ships run by the Holland America Line. There is the large number of Indonesian staff on board, as well as classical and modern Dutch art. To fit out the interior of the MS Rotterdam, five VFD employees, with a budget of three million dollars, searched auctions worldwide for classical Dutch arts and crafts. The preference in this regard was for objects with a maritime connection such as an original 17th century bronze VOC cannon from a Hoorn merchant ship. However, every now and again the appearance is deceptive. Take the huge 16th century style painting entitled 'View of the Port of Amsterdam at the Singel Canal' hanging in the Explorers Lounge, for example. This was only produced in 1997, painted by the English trompe l'oeil specialist, Ian Cairnie.

Many, but not all of the works of art are related to shipping or to the Netherlands. Fine examples of this include the Chinese bronze sculpture of a horse from the Han Dynasty or the Japanese Samurai armour from the 17th century. Time is one of the themes on board and situated in the atrium is the eye-catching nine metre high Times Square, an enormous Flemish clock with fourteen time zones and an astrolabe. Although it looks antique, it was specially designed for the Rotterdam by Italian artists Gilbert Lebigre and Corinne Roger. On top is the figure of Hercules (not Atlas, as many people mistakenly believe) holding up the sky.

The Holland America Line is rightly proud of its art collection, with some of the art work has a museum quality. Art lovers on board can obtain information at reception to attend the Art & Antique Tour and view all of the works of art on board — a bit like visiting a museum. An audio tour can even be downloaded via the website to play on an iPod or MP3 device before embarking. This audio tour is complemented by interviews with specialists such as the architect Dingemans and a number of artists.

The blend of modern and classical art and stylish, comfortable décor give the MS Rotterdam its own special identity. Combined with the excellent service on board, it is a worthy successor to its reputable predecessors.

VENICE

Arriving in Venice by cruise ship with a view of the magnificent churches and palazzos is an unforgettable experience. The city owes its wealth and opulence, reflected in the architecture, to the water. The maritime history of Venice can be seen in the Museo Storico Navale (Historical Naval Museum) and the Arsenale, both within walking distance of St. Mark's Square.

If there is one city that is linked to the water, it is Venice. Built on a patchwork of islands, the city owes its wealth to that water; in the glory days, Venice was, thanks to its fleet, the most powerful republic of the region.

The best way to to see the city's maritime history is to walk in an easterly direction from St. Mark's Square via the Riva degli Schiavoni promenade. While walking along the Canale di San Marco, you have a lovely view of the San Giorgo Maggiore church, one of the best-known buildings in the city. On the waterfront is the Museo Storico Navale where the maritime history of Venice is beautifully showcased. There are even original boats to admire, such as a gondola belonging to the legendary Peggy Guggenheim.

Behind the museum is the Arsenale, the former shipyard (and munitions depot) of the city, protected by crenelated walls. The shipyard dates back to the 12th century. At its peak in the 16th century, there were 16,000 men working there and it was the largest shipyard in the world. In fact, it was a city within a city, with its own shops, workshops and factories where galleys were built in a sort of assembly line system. With these ships, Venice was able to monopolise trade in the Mediterranean and thus amass great wealth.

The Arsenale is now managed by the navy, with entire sections standing empty; some buildings are used as exhibition areas, as for the Biennale, for example.

Two square towers stand out to the left and right of the waterfront. There used to be two huge doors between these towers to close off the shipyard and protect it against any attacks from the water. Now the doors are gone, access is open to local shipping. The gateway from 1460, protected by two giant lions (plundered from the Greek Piraeus in 1687), is regarded as the first Renaissance structure in Venice.

Anyone strolling around the tranquil neighbourhood near the Arsenale will soon discover the day-to-day life of the city. It is fascinating that you can experience the leisurely pace of everyday Venetian life such a short distance from the constant hustle and bustle of all the tourists around St. Mark's Square.

CRYSTAL SERENITY

The abundance of facilities on a large ship combined with the luxury, service and intimacy of a small ship. That is precisely the recipe that makes Crystal Serenity one of the top cruise ships of its time.

The first thing that strikes you on board is the vast amount of space. You would never think for one moment that you are on a ship with more than 1,000 other passengers. On the contrary, the peace and quiet you expect on small ships prevails throughout the entire vessel. That's because the Crystal Serenity has one of the highest passenger/space ratio of all the current cruise ships.

Something else that stands out is the relatively large number of Japanese on board. But this is not so surprising, given that the Japanese Nippon Yusen Kaisha (NYK) is an owner and parent company of Crystal Cruises. NYK is one of the largest container transporters in the world: in addition to a fleet of over 800 ships, it also has aircraft, trains and trucks. In 1988, it was decided to set up Crystal Cruises with the aim of setting new standards of luxury in the international cruise industry.

In contrast to the parent company, the Crystal fleet is very modest, comprising just two vessels. In addition to the Serenity with a capacity of 1,070 passengers, there is only the smaller Crystal Symphony, which can accommodate 922 guests. In 2006, the Crystal Harmony was withdrawn from the Japanese market, sold and rechristened the Asuka II.

With an international clientele, Serenity has travelled all over the world since her debut in 2003. The emphasis of the all-inclusive ship is on 'wining and dining'. In addition to the centrally located Crystal Dining Room, there are two speciality restaurants: the Italian Prego and the Asian Silk Roads. Here, too, you can find the Japanese influence since Silk Roads is under the supervision of none other than the legendary Japanese chef Nobuyuki 'Nobu' Matsuhisa. There is even a Nobu Sushi Bar, the only floating Nobu branch in the world. There is no extra charge for dining in the speciality restaurants. It also goes without saying that the quality of the food in all of the restaurants is sublime. Rarely will you have eaten such delicious food.

Together with the Lido Café, Trident Grill, The Vintage Room, Tastes and room service (where you can also order from the menu of the various restaurants), there is a wealth of dining possibilities every day. The Serenity has all the usual amenities of a large cruise ship, such as a spa (fitted out according to the Feng Shui principles), a casino, various shops, bars, a show lounge (where there are excellent free lectures on various subjects) and a cinema. Other impressive facilities include the Avenue Saloon, furnished in the style of a gentlemen's club, and the Connoisseurs Club with its colonial style atmosphere, the venue for avid cigar smokers. More athletic guests can enjoy the Serenity's swimming pools, whirlpools, fitness room, paddle tennis courts, golf simulator and driving range.

Helsinki, 2 August. Went to the spa today. Maria, the stunning Venezuelan therapist, took things seriously. The initial interview was thorough and the Thai Herbal Massage was wonderfully relaxing. On Maria's advice, I then spent 30 minutes in the steam bath. After that, she wrote down all kinds of advice for me to use on my return to the Netherlands. It's really wonderful to be treated by such a professional therapists! Back in my room, the butler, Vincente, appeared to have brought in some healthy snacks. Finally fell asleep on the reclining chair on my veranda after a glass of champagne. I think I'll just take a dip in my Jacuzzi...

'We wanted modern classical elegance. We wanted Fifth Avenue crème de la crème, New York-inspired living and retail spaces that people love and look forward to spending time in.' These are the words of Keith Rushbrook from Canadese II by IV Design. This architectural firm is partly responsible for the Serenity's recent 52 million dollar refurbishment that has given the ship a new, fresh look.

Particularly special is the Promenade Deck for walkers and joggers. Here they can get some fresh air undisturbed and unhindered by obstacles like sun beds as is often the case on other cruise ships. Daily walks are organised with professional guidance.

The many returning guests to the Serenity and the numerous awards won by the cruise company (no other cruise operator, hotel or resort has won as many 'World's Best' prizes) is testimony that blending the attributes of a large ship with those of a small ship creates a perfect cruise experience. The outstanding service provided by the well-trained personnel and the excellent food have become legendary in the world of cruising. It is clear that the goal Crystal set itself in 1988 has been achieved with flying colours.

SS
ROTTERDAM

Rotterdam is the perfect place for those who don't want to sail the seas but would like to experience the atmosphere of a cruise ship. That is where the former flagship of the Holland-America Line in the 1950's bearing the same name is now permanently moored at the quayside, serving as a hotel, entertainment and congress centre.

Over the years, the Holland-America Line, abbreviated to HAL, has given the name 'Rotterdam' to several ships. It is a tribute to the cruise operator's home port. The steamship (SS) Rotterdam is the fifth vessel with this name and is therefore followed by the Roman numeral V or 5.

Back in 1938, there were already plans to build a new ship to operate alongside the New Amsterdam (II). However, these plans were abandoned as a result of the uncertain political situation in Europe and the outbreak of World War II. The keel of construction number 300 was finally laid on 14 December 1956 at the Rotterdamsche Droogdok Maatschappij (RDM) shipyard. During the christening and launch by Queen Juliana on 13 September 1958, it became evident just how popular the ship was. The audience, some ten thousand strong, stood several rows deep on both banks to enjoy the spectacle. A year later, on 3 September 1959, SS Rotterdam set course on her maiden voyage to New York, with Princess Beatrix on board as the guest of honour.

For that time, the Rotterdam was a ship of superlatives. 'The ship of tomorrow... today' was its advertising slogan. The ship has a very luxurious interior as well as two elegant and innovative funnels which made her instantly recognisable.

The SS Rotterdam, 228 metres in length, is the largest passenger ship ever constructed in the Netherlands. She was built for both cruise activities and the transatlantic crossing; the latter required additional specifications, including a slender and raised bow. There was both a 1st class and a tourist class, separated from each other horizontally by an ingenious double staircase and removable partitions. This made it easy to turn the vessel into a single-class cruise ship when necessary. During its first ten years, the ship operated regularly on the transatlantic route between Rotterdam and New York from April to December and was used for cruises after that. The Rotterdam returned from her final transatlantic crossing on 3 October 1968. She was then refitted at RDM and deployed as a full-time cruise ship.

On 6 October 1971, the vessel departed on her final transatlantic trip from Rotterdam to New York. The name Holland-America Line was used for many decades to emphasise the company's international character. From 1973 to the mid-1980s, the shipping company called itself Holland America Cruises.

In 1989, the Holland-America Line was taken over by the American Carnival Cruise Lines. The Rotterdam was subsequently sold in 1997 to another American company, Premier Cruises. In the same year, the ship completed the last of her thirty world cruises, a voyage that lasted about 80 days. The Rotterdam was then rechristened the Rembrandt, a tribute to the ship's Dutch roots. Premier Cruises was declared bankrupt in 2000 and the Rembrandt was laid up in Freeport on the island of Grand Bahama.

The graceful lady of the sea was threatened with demolition, but this was prevented by RDM's purchase of the vessel in 2003 for a price of around three million euro. A year later, she was towed to Gibraltar for renovations. She then got back her old name and home port. Via Cadiz in Spain, where the Rotterdam was repainted in her original colours (the hull had been painted dark blue over the years), her journey continued to Gdansk in Poland for extensive restoration. However, the Polish authorities were very slow to issue a permit, partly due to the presence of asbestos and because protected swallows had nested on board. For months, the Rotterdam lay neglected at the wharf. Eventually, in August, she was moved to Wilhelmshaven in northern Germany, where work began on restoring and renovating the vessel. On 4 August 2008, the 'Grand Dame' returned to her birthplace, where she moored at the quay at 3ᵉ Katendrechtsehoofd.

The restoration had been completed but there was a hefty price to pay: the estimated budget had been grossly exceeded, mainly due to the complexity of the project. Fortunately, the result was something to be proud of and the ship became a unique attraction in the city of Rotterdam.

Those who now go aboard the ship will be charmed by the 1950s style. Only the Lido has a more contemporary look with modern furniture and its openwork ceiling, exposing the piping.

Not all areas are freely accessible, but there is an audio tour for visiting the most important areas (including the bridge and the captain's cabin).

One of the best preserved rooms is the Ambassador Room on the Upper Promenade Deck, which was only accessible to first-class passengers during scheduled services back then. This room, as well as the ingenious double staircase, were designed by the Amsterdam architect Han van Tienhoven, who also designed the furniture in the Ambassador Room. The heavyweight lounge chairs prevented them from shifting during heavy weather at sea.

The company tried to preserve as many of the original elements as possible during the renovation, although much had been lost over the years, such as the tapestries in the Club Room. Fortunately, the designer, Gisèle d'Ailly-van Waterschoot van der Gracht, still had the original designs and was able to weave the tapestries again. It is good to see that the Holland-America Line attached such great importance to the interior of the ship and to the comfort of the passengers.

The art of travel is to enjoy every day, every hour, every minute you spend on the way to your destination. And this was certainly the case on the magnificent steamship Rotterdam. And she can still be enjoyed even though she no longer sails.

L·XL

LARGE AND MEGA SHIPS

L·XL

When Royal Caribbean's Sovereign of the Seas (capacity 2,276 passengers) began her maiden voyage from Miami in 1988, it set the tone for cruising as many of us know it today. The ship itself was the destination. It was a sort of floating holiday park, the first cruise ship designed for mass tourism. Since then, many more of these so-called 'floating resorts' have been built. They are not just big (with a capacity of between 1,751 and 4,000 passengers), but also provide a wealth of recreational opportunities. Obviously all vessels of this type feature swimming pools, usually with slides, whirlpools, spas, theatres, cinemas, shopping galleries, tennis courts, basketball courts, ice rinks, climbing walls, miniature golf courses, golf simulators, and of course several bars, discos, restaurants and casinos. In short, they are well-equipped sailing holiday villages with the captain as mayor.

The interiors of some of the newer big ships would not look out of place in Las Vegas, with the 'experience architecture' in the exuberant ships of Carnival Cruise Lines – designed by Joe Farcus – taking the crown. Here, all kinds of design styles seem to have been blended together and then strewn across the ship. One bar, in the style of ancient Egypt, is next to a high-tech sports bar with a host of flat-screen TVs showing non-stop videos clips and sporting events. The atriums, the showpieces of such ships, are almost like modern cathedrals in which neon-decorated lifts shoot up and down.

Other companies, such as Cunard with its Queen Mary 2, feed off their rich maritime history. They continue to build ships with lots of dark wood, shiny brass and various references to Art Deco, the style of the Golden Age of ocean liners. Celebrity Cruises gives its ships a modern and contemporary interior. It is also constantly inventing new and original attractions with which to lure customers. On the newest ships it is even possible to picnic on the outside deck on – yes – a real lawn.

Ships like Royal Caribbean's Oasis of the Seas represent a new category of cruising: the XL or mega-cruise ships (over 4,000 passengers). The Oasis of the Seas can carry more than 6,000 guests. A week seems a really short amount of time in which to admire all the attractions. It is the first ship in the world with a real park on board: the 100m long Central Park is home to 12,000 plants in addition to 27 real trees.

Large and mega-ships are, by definition, not exclusive. Ultimately they are destined for mass tourism. But on some of these ships certain companies have created, in the best locations, exclusive VIP sections that are out-of-bounds to 'standard' cruisers. One such example is Norwegian Cruise Line's The Haven. MSC Cruises has the Yacht Club, where guests are pampered by well-trained personnel serving them in stylish evening dress. The advantage of this concept is that you can still have all the fun and entertainment of a huge ship, but can escape the crowds and withdraw to an exclusive club, with swimming pool, whirlpool, restaurant, lounge and bar. A great concept, especially for families whose children have interests that differ from their parents.' For many, the additional cost is money well spent.

QUEEN MARY 2

The Queen Mary 2, the largest ocean liner ever, is the latest in a long line of legendary Cunard ships. This lady has been specially designed to defy the often stormy Atlantic.

The history of transatlantic crossings began in 1838. The British government decided in that year that a regular shipping link needed to be established between England and Halifax in Canada providing, amongst other things, a postal service. The contract eventually went to Samuel Cunard who in 1840 launched the service. It was a success, and in 1863 a second route (Liverpool-New York) was added.

Other cruise lines, including White Star Line, observed the success of the Cunard Line and launched competing services. Eventually the two companies were forced to merge in 1934 for financial reasons, and the Cunard White Star Line was born. Two years later, the now legendary ocean liner Queen Mary went into service.

In the late 1950s, the company changed its name back to Cunard Line. With the advent of air travel in the 1960s, it became more viable for Cunard to concentrate on offering cruises instead of transatlantic crossings. When Cunard was taken over by America's Carnival Cruise Lines in 1998, people asked whether another ocean liner would ever be built. Fortunately, this uncertainty was removed in 2000 with the announcement of the Queen Mary 2, known as QM2, successor to the Queen Elizabeth 2. She went into service just four years later, with the intention of providing both cruises and

transatlantic crossings. Her bow was reinforced and her engines were upgraded to over 170,000 horsepower.

A transatlantic crossing is a special experience. Days at sea, with no land in sight, gives the feeling of adventure and space with a different rhythm. It is pleasant to be a guest on a luxury ship like the QM2.

345 metres long and 150,000 tonnes, it is nearly twice as large as its predecessor – the Queen Mary. It is also more than 100 times larger than the wooden ship the Britannia, with which Samuel Cunard launched his first transatlantic service.

On average, 42,000 cups of tea and 112,000 meals are served on a single crossing and a rather respectable 2,400 bottles of champagne are uncorked. Every day more than 1,000 bottles of wine are taken from the world's largest floating wine cellar.

The interior, though designed by Swedish interior designer Robert Tillberg, has an English atmosphere and features extensive use of dark wood and heavy carpets. The interior design also points to the rich past of ocean liners: subtle reminders of the past are seen everywhere, with many appropriate Art Deco touches. The Grand Lobby is the stylish centre of the ship. The monumental bas-relief with 1930s elements, by Scotsman John McKenna, that hangs high in the lobby is a real eye-catcher.

In the Britannia restaurant, which extends over three floors, tapestry art at key focal points gives an Art Deco atmosphere. The work of Dutch artist Barbara Broekman hangs prominently above the Captain's table. The Britannia can accommodate as many as 1,347 guests at a time. Although there are no class distinctions on board, only guests in the more expensive suites are allowed to dine in the QM2's top restaurant, the Queen's Grill.

As an English liner, it is not without a traditional English pub, the Golden Lion, just one of the fourteen bars on-board. The Queen Mary 2 is the only cruise ship to have a special deck with a kennel and dog groomer. There is even a lamppost against which every dog can pee in its customary position!

There is plenty to do during a transatlantic crossing, and none of the 2,620 guests needs be bored for a moment. Pools, bars, restaurants, a spa, a cinema, various shops, a hyper-modern disco (called G32, after the shipyard construction number given to the QM2) a planetarium and the world's largest floating library (8,500 titles), all of which provide more than adequate distraction.

The Promenade Deck invites you to walk in the fresh air or even go jogging – if only to burn off the extra ingested calories.

During each crossing lectures are given on a particular theme by various guest speakers, who are always specialists in their field. These lectures are generally of such high quality and interest that people book crossings especially in order to attend them.

New York, 16 May. Arrived today in the Big Apple. What a spectacular entry! It had already been announced that we would be passing by the Statue of Liberty at around half past six, so everyone was up and about early. On deck it was very busy. Everyone was there taking pictures or filming, and we all cheered enthusiastically as the Statue of Liberty came into view. Suddenly I realized that I was standing and experiencing one end of a very long tradition. How many immigrants in the past, looking for a new future, must have been delighted at the sight of this statue? But under far less luxurious conditions...

A transatlantic crossing is a perfect way to unwind. Days pass at sea without the distraction of a port of call. The view of the vast ocean, the fresh air; it all has a very relaxing effect. Anyone sailing from Europe to New York also gains a massive bonus: as the ship passes through five time zones, you are treated to an extra hour's sleep on five days of the crossing. A very pleasant way to avoid jet lag. Travelling to America in this traditional way also gives you a better sense of distance, time, and maritime history.

CELEBRITY REFLECTION

Modern Luxury. Celebrity Cruises' attention-grabbing slogan, is aptly chosen. Guests aboard the trendy Celebrity Reflection can immerse themselves in all kinds of luxury.

For brothers John and Michael Chandris, 1989 was their year. Cruising was becoming increasingly popular, making it the the right time to set up a contemporary European-oriented cruise line offering great quality at a reasonable price. Along with fellow Greek Harry Haralambopoulos the London cargo vessel owners enthusiastically set to work, and Celebrity Cruises was born. The cruise line was so successful that in 1997 US corporation Royal Caribbean International acquired the company for a nifty 1.3 billion dollars.

Celebrity's ships are easily recognizable by the large 'X' on the funnel. But why an 'X'? This letter 'chi', the second but last letter of the Greek alphabet, and pronounced 'ch' in English, is the first letter of the surname of the company's founders in Greek.

The Celebrity fleet consists of ships of various sizes. The smallest, the Celebrity Xpedition, is a boutique ship with room for only 96 guests, operating all year around the Galapagos Islands. Then there is the Celebrity Century, with a capacity of 1,814 passengers, and a further four identical vessels sailing in the slightly larger Millennium class (1,950 passengers). Finally, there is the five-ship Solstice Class, accommodating 3,030 passengers, and includes the existing Celebrity Reflection vessels.

New York-based design firm BG Studio International designed the modern interior of the Celebrity Reflection and all the other ships owned by Celebrity. Its founders are Italian architect Francesca Bucci and Australian designer Hans Galutera (a magna cum laude graduate of the Fashion Institute of Technology in New York) . Both have many years' experience of designing hip hotels, contemporary Manhattan penthouses and trendy cruise ships. They take great pride in delivering atmospheric interior designs that do something to you. The firm describes its style of decorating as 'Urbane simplicity; relaxed New York sophistication, punctuated by precise European attention to detail'.

The duo has gone to great lengths to give the Celebrity Reflection's passengers a sense of space with high, airy, naturally-lit rooms finished in a contemporary style. The result is a particularly attractive, modern and stylish interior.

On a ship with more than 3,000 passengers, it is important that you can occasionally find a quiet spot, away from your cabin or suite. Celebrity Reflection fills this need with its various facilities where guests can escape from the crowd. The Hideaway is a good example: this large two-story room contains egg-shaped plastic seating elements into which passengers can retire and remain undisturbed. For couples wanting to cocoon in shared solitude there are metre-high wooden egg-shaped skeletons with double sofas.

At the back of the outside deck there is further evidence that Celebrity Cruises is a modern and fashionable cruise line, with several shady covered cabanas, known as 'The Alcoves'. These lounge areas can be rented and offer privacy for up to four guests. An iPad is loaded with movies, magazines, music and games ready for use. There is also a WiFi connection. Food, snacks, and drinks are provided in a stylish picnic basket.

The Alcoves are on the edge of The Lawn Club, a genuine lawn ideal for picnics, sunbathing or croquet. A lawn this pristine does not just grow on its own: the liner's owners have brought in a team of landscape architects and irrigation and soil specialists to make the Lawn Club a success.

It has proven to be a popular venue for many passengers, perhaps because it is so unusual and worth experiencing at least once. The sight of a gardener cutting grass with an electric mower on a ship's deck is, well, a little incongruous.

At sea, 12 October. Early this morning, couldn't resist going to the rear deck. I was one of the first. Comfortable temperature and a gentle sun. After my first cup of coffee of the day I kicked off my flip-flops to walk across the lawn. It's weird to feel grass under your feet while you're at sea. Marvellous! Then it was lovely to read the paper, stretched out on the grass with a blade of it in my mouth.

The Lawn Club Grill, an open air grill where as a guest you can grill your own meat, is also situated on this unusual deck. The chef is there to offer guidance, if you want it, and it is just one of twelve dining options on board.

The variety of these eating opportunities is huge and the quality of the food very good. The large and beautifully-designed Opus is the main restaurant, seating up to 1,454 guests. Another all-inclusive eatery is the trendy Qsine fun-food restaurant, seating just 92 guests, where food is presented in an original way – sushi in the form of a lollipop! The very height of modernity, the digital menu is actually on an iPad, with pictures and videos to help you choose your meal, and with which you signal your choice through to the kitchen. Whilst the food here is included in the cruise price, this does not apply to the exclusive Blu restaurant, with its cool white and blue interior. Still unimpressed? Michael's Club, aboard the Celebrity Reflection, offers no less than 64 different beers. The Martini Bar & Crush, with a frozen counter as an eye-catching attraction, has more than 100 types of vodka on the drinks list. For those who still find this all too mundane, there is the Molecular Bar, where the cocktail list features spectacular cocktails – some of which are prepared using liquid nitrogen.

The attention to detail on board the ship is striking and extends beyond the meticulous design. The service is friendly, informal and light-hearted in the traditional American way. Everything is equally stylish, contemporary and well thought out. And with such a varied range of entertainments on offer, it is impossible to get bored on this ship. Celebrity Cruises believes that every moment of an on-board vacation should be extraordinary. And they make sure it is. Real Modern Luxury.

AMSTERDAM

Half an hour's walk from the Amsterdam Passenger Terminal is the former treasury of the Admiralty of Amsterdam. This sturdy building is now the Maritime Museum.

It is 1658. Amsterdam is the trading centre of the world. The Republic of the United Netherlands has a strong fleet and thus unquestionably rules the waves. In particular the Dutch East India Company, the world's first truly multinational company, brings great wealth into the country off the back of a roaring spice trade. A warehouse is needed to store all those valuable goods brought in from the East.

Amsterdam city architect Daniel Stalpaert has been commissioned to design the 's Lands Zeemagazijn. For this, he designed a square building in a sober, classical style with a large open courtyard designed to store goods. Brought into use in 1656, it immediately became a popular tourist attraction. The building is located on what was then the outskirts of Amsterdam. From the top floor visitors can enjoy superb views of the city on one side, and the IJ and the many ships on the other. Although a fierce fire in 1791 destroyed much of the building, the thick outer walls remained standing and the Zeemagazijn was later restored to its former glory.

It was only in 1973 that it was deemed to no longer meet the needs of the day and the Navy (the successor to the Admiralty) moved its activities to another location. It was at this point that the Maritime Museum then settled in the Zeemagazijn.

Re-opening again in 2011 after a lengthy four-year renovation, the museum features one of the largest maritime collections in the world, with no less than 300,000 paintings, globes, ship models, instruments and other items exhibited in modern surroundings.

The museum contains an actual replica of the Dutch East India Company's East Indiaman Amsterdam. The original ship hit bad weather during its maiden voyage in 1749, sinking off the coast of England near Hastings. Its cargo included 27 boxes of silver, with a value of around 300,000 guilders, the equivalent today of several million dollars. Understandably the wreck has attracted treasure-hunters ever since.

The replica, built in African teak, was completed in 1990. The 48-metre-long vessel (measured from bowsprit to stern) was built by 400 volunteers and is open to the public.

MSC FANTASIA YACHT CLUB

A ship in a ship. Or the cruising equivalent to the business class top deck of a Boeing 747. This is how MSC Cruises describes its Yacht Club concept. One thing is certain: anyone booking a suite in the Yacht Club gets the best of both worlds, with the luxury and comfort of an exclusive club and the facilities of a large modern cruise ship.

Anyone booking a holiday in the Yacht Club enjoys numerous privileges. The journey begins with relaxed priority boarding. After being welcomed aboard by friendly staff, in an area screened off from the ship's other passengers, the luxury begins. A butler, available 24 hours a day, can unpack your suitcase for you upon request. Each suite features a well-stocked minibar that is refilled daily. The exclusive restaurant and lounge serve select beverages such as wine and champagne free of charge.

The MSC Fantasia is one of the largest ships ever built for the European market. The figures alone are impressive: in addition to space for 4,363 passengers, there is room for 1,300 crew members. Of the 1,637 cabins, 71 are for the Yacht Club. Besides the Fantasia, only the MSC Preziosa, MSC Divina MSC Splendida include the premium VIP Yacht Clubs.

Piraeus, 5 September. It was a shock when I saw the MSC Fantasia for real. What a huge ship! The check-in, accompanied by my butler, went ahead really fast. Before I knew it I was in the Top Sail Lounge with a glass of chilled white wine in my hand. With a beautiful view as a bonus. I think this is going to be my favourite hang-out spot...

The numbers of the parent company are awe-inspiring. The Mediterranean Shipping Company was founded in 1970 by Captain Gianluigi Aponte. At the time, the company consisted of a single ship trading between Africa and Sorrento (the birthplace). Today MSC is the world's second largest containership undertaking, with a fleet of 474 ships. MSC Cruises was created in 1989 with the acquisition of Flotta Lauro. Daughter Alexa and son Diego worked for the cruise side of the business, along with their mother Rafaela. She is responsible for the design of the ships in typical Italian glamour style, with her friend Sophia Loren helping her out occasionally! The MSC Divina even has a Sophia Loren Royal Suite, designed by the famous movie star, with walls adorned with photos of the diva in some of her famous roles. A replica of her dressing table allows guests in this suite to feel like a movie star or like Sophia Loren herself, who is also patron of the MSC cruise fleet.

The Yacht Club is located on decks 15 and 16, the most attractive location of the ship, and is directly above the Aurea Spa to which it is attached. In addition to its own sundeck with bar, pool and whirlpools, the Yacht Club offers a reception hall with seating area, an open-plan restaurant, a small library and a panoramic lounge. In this Top Sail Lounge, the central part of the Yacht Club, an exquisite buffet with varied and delectable snacks is open all day long. The view from this observation lounge is perfect, as is the impeccable service of the butlers in their formal dress.

Yacht Club members even have their own priority lifts: placing their card in a special reader gives them priority over ordinary passengers. Another perk of being a special guest!

Dubrovnik, 7 September. Dinner today for six after the theatre show. Fantastic! Mixed entertainment with acrobatics, trapeze and very high quality singing. Pity it was all over in just 45 minutes. After the show we enjoyed delicious food at L'Etoile, and then we wandered around the ship a bit and downed some drinks in the Manhattan Bar. Later in the evening it got quite busy and the whole group agreed to have a nightcap in the Top Sail Lounge, as it's a good place to sit quietly. It was so comfortable there that we ended up staying longer than originally planned. Well, that's what holidays are for...

A large ship like the MSC Fantasia has a lot of entertainment on offer, which on the one hand is nice but on the other hand it can all get a bit noisy and too much. So what could be nicer than to be able to retreat to one's own exclusive club? People travelling with children will certainly appreciate this concept, as the kids can have fun at the disco, the large pool or the Formula 1 simulator while their parents enjoy a cocktail in the ONE Bar located on the Yacht Club sun deck.

The service is excellent. Little things show that MSC takes this concept very seriously. Take, for example, the wide variety of pillows to chose from. Once you have chosen from the 'pillow' menu, you simply call the butler and your pillow is delivered to your room. As a guest in the Yacht Club you can also specify which newspaper you want to read. The same-day edition of the selected newspaper will be printed on board and delivered directly to your suite. And not just a summary on a few A4 sheets; no, a personalized tabloid version of the entire newspaper. It's this kind of detail that makes a stay in the Yacht Club so pleasant.

TECHNICAL INFORMATION

BOUTIQUE SHIPS

SEA CLOUD

39.5
PASSENGER/SPACE RATIO

1.1
CREW/PASSENGER RATIO

TONNAGE	2532
LENGTH/BEAM/DRAFT (IN METRES)	109.5/14.9/5.1
COMMISSIONED IN	1931
NUMBER OF PASSENGER DECKS	3
NUMBER OF PASSENGERS	64
CREW	60
NUMBER OF CABINS	32

SEA CLOUD
WWW.SEACLOUD.COM

SILVER EXPLORER

46
PASSENGER/SPACE RATIO

1.2
CREW/PASSENGER RATIO

TONNAGE	6072
LENGTH/BEAM/DRAFT (IN METRES)	108/15.9/4.3
COMMISSIONED (AS THE PRINCE ALBERT II) IN	1989
NUMBER OF PASSENGER DECKS	5
NUMBER OF PASSENGERS	132
CREW	111
NUMBER OF CABINS	66

SILVERSEA CRUISES
WWW.SILVERSEA.COM/EXPEDITIONS/

STAR FLYER

13.5
PASSENGER/SPACE RATIO

2.3
CREW/PASSENGER RATIO

TONNAGE	2298
LENGTH/BEAM/DRAFT (IN METRES)	109.7/15.2/5.6
COMMISSIONED IN	1991
NUMBER OF PASSENGER DECKS	4
NUMBER OF PASSENGERS	170
CREW	72
NUMBER OF CABINS	85

STAR CLIPPERS
WWW.STARCLIPPERS.COM

SEADREAM II

38.7
PASSENGER/SPACE RATIO

1.2
CREW/PASSENGER RATIO

TONNAGE	4333
LENGTH/BEAM/DRAFT (IN METRES)	104.8/14.6/4.1
COMMISSIONED (AS THE SEA GODDESS II) IN	1985
NUMBER OF PASSENGER DECKS	5
NUMBER OF PASSENGERS	112
CREW	95
NUMBER OF CABINS	54

SEADREAM YACHT CLUB
WWW.SEADREAM.COM

SMALL SHIPS

ROYAL CLIPPER

22.1
PASSENGER/SPACE RATIO

2.2
CREW/PASSENGER RATIO

TONNAGE	5061
LENGTH/BEAM/DRAFT (IN METRES)	133.8/16.5/5.6
COMMISSIONED (AS THE SEA GODDESS II) IN	2000
NUMBER OF PASSENGER DECKS	5
NUMBER OF PASSENGERS	228
CREW	106
NUMBER OF CABINS	114

STAR CLIPPERS
WWW.STARCLIPPERS.COM

EUROPA 2

85.7
PASSENGER/SPACE RATIO

1.4
CREW/PASSENGER RATIO

TONNAGE	42.830
LENGTH/BEAM/DRAFT (IN METRES)	225.4/26.7/6.3
COMMISSIONED IN	2013
NUMBER OF PASSENGER DECKS	7
NUMBER OF PASSENGERS	500
CREW	370
NUMBER OF CABINS	251

HAPAG LLOYD CRUISES
WWW.HL-CRUISES.COM

NAUTICA

44.2
PASSENGER/SPACE RATIO

1.8
CREW/PASSENGER RATIO

TONNAGE	30.277
LENGTH/BEAM/DRAFT (IN METRES)	180.9/25.5/5.9
COMMISSIONED (AS THE R FIVE) IN	1998
NUMBER OF PASSENGER DECKS	9
NUMBER OF PASSENGERS	684
CREW	386
NUMBER OF CABINS	342

OCEANIA CRUISES
WWW.OCEANIACRUISES.COM

WIND SURF

47.6
PASSENGER/SPACE RATIO

1.6
CREW/PASSENGER RATIO

TONNAGE	14.745
LENGTH/BEAM/DRAFT (IN METRES)	187/20/5
COMMISSIONED (AS THE CLUB MED I) IN	1990
NUMBER OF PASSENGER DECKS	7
NUMBER OF PASSENGERS	310
CREW	191
NUMBER OF CABINS	156

WINDSTAR CRUISES
WWW.WINDSTARCRUISES.COM

LE BORÉAL / L'AUSTRAL

40.5 / 41.5
PASSENGER/SPACE RATIO

1.9
CREW/PASSENGER RATIO

TONNAGE LE BORÉAL/L'AUSTRAL	10.700/10.944
LENGTH/BEAM/DRAFT (IN METRES)	142/18/4.7
COMMISSIONED IN	2010/2011
NUMBER OF PASSENGER DECKS	6
NUMBER OF PASSENGERS	264
CREW	139
NUMBER OF CABINS	132

COMPAGNIE DU PONANT
WWW.PONANT.COM

SEABOURN SOJOURN

71.1
PASSENGER/SPACE RATIO

1.4
CREW/PASSENGER RATIO

TONNAGE	32.000
LENGTH/BEAM/DRAFT (IN METRES)	198.1/25.6/6.5
COMMISSIONED IN	2010
NUMBER OF PASSENGER DECKS	10
NUMBER OF PASSENGERS	450
CREW	330
NUMBER OF CABINS	225

SEABOURN
WWW.SEABOURN.COM

SEVEN SEAS VOYAGER

59.8
PASSENGER/SPACE RATIO

1.6
CREW/PASSENGER RATIO

TONNAGE	42.363
LENGTH/BEAM/DRAFT (IN METRES)	204/28.8/7
COMMISSIONED IN	2003
NUMBER OF PASSENGER DECKS	9
NUMBER OF PASSENGERS	708
CREW	447
NUMBER OF CABINS	354

REGENT SEVEN SEAS CRUISES
WWW.RSSC.COM

SILVER CLOUD

56.8
PASSENGER/SPACE RATIO

1.3
CREW/PASSENGER RATIO

TONNAGE	16.800
LENGTH/BEAM/DRAFT (IN METRES)	156.7/21.5/5.3
COMMISSIONED IN	1994
NUMBER OF PASSENGER DECKS	6
NUMBER OF PASSENGERS	296
CREW	222
NUMBER OF CABINS	148

SILVERSEA CRUISES
WWW.SILVERSEA.COM

MID-SIZED SHIPS

RIVIERA

52.7
PASSENGER/SPACE RATIO

1.6
CREW/PASSENGER RATIO

TONNAGE	66.084
LENGTH/BEAM/DRAFT (IN METRES)	239.2/32.2/7.3
COMMISSIONED IN	2012
NUMBER OF PASSENGER DECKS	11
NUMBER OF PASSENGERS	1250
CREW	800
NUMBER OF CABINS	625

OCEANIA CRUISES
WWW.OCEANIACRUISES.COM

MS ROTTERDAM

44
PASSENGER/SPACE RATIO

2.3
CREW/PASSENGER RATIO

TONNAGE	61.849
LENGTH/BEAM/DRAFT (IN METRES)	237.7/32.2/7.8
COMMISSIONED IN	1997
NUMBER OF PASSENGER DECKS	12
NUMBER OF PASSENGERS	1404
CREW	600
NUMBER OF CABINS	702

HOLLAND AMERICA LINE
NL.HOLLANDAMERICA.COM – WWW.HOLLANDAMERICA.COM

CRYSTAL SERENITY

64.4
PASSENGER/SPACE RATIO

1.6
CREW/PASSENGER RATIO

TONNAGE	68.870
LENGTH/BEAM/DRAFT (IN METRES)	250/32.2/7.6
COMMISSIONED IN	2003
NUMBER OF PASSENGER DECKS	9
NUMBER OF PASSENGERS	1070
CREW	655
NUMBER OF CABINS	535

CRYSTAL CRUISES
WWW.CRYSTALCRUISES.COM

SS ROTTERDAM

26.6
PASSENGER/SPACE RATIO

1.9
CREW/PASSENGER RATIO

TONNAGE	38.645
LENGTH/BEAM/DRAFT (IN METRES)	228.1/28.6/9
COMMISSIONED IN	1959
NUMBER OF PASSENGER DECKS	8
NUMBER OF PASSENGERS	1456
CREW	776
NUMBER OF CABINS ORIGINALLY / NOW	576/254

HOLLAND AMERIKA LIJN
WWW.SSROTTERDAM.NL

LARGE AND MEGA SHIPS

QUEEN MARY 2

58.4
PASSENGER/SPACE RATIO

2.1
CREW/PASSENGER RATIO

TONNAGE	151.400
LENGTH/BEAM/DRAFT (IN METRES)	344.4/41.1/9.8
COMMISSIONED IN	2004
NUMBER OF PASSENGER DECKS	14
NUMBER OF PASSENGERS	2592
CREW	1253
NUMBER OF CABINS	1296

CUNARD LINE
WWW.CUNARD.COM

CELEBRITY REFLECTION

41.6
PASSENGER/SPACE RATIO

2.4
CREW/PASSENGER RATIO

TONNAGE	126.000
LENGTH/BEAM/DRAFT (IN METRES)	319.1/37.5/8.2
COMMISSIONED IN	2012
NUMBER OF PASSENGER DECKS	13
NUMBER OF PASSENGERS	3030
CREW	1255
NUMBER OF CABINS	1523

CELEBRITY CRUISES
WWW.AMCA.NL/CELEBRITY-CRUISES – WWW.CELEBRITYCRUISES.COM

MSC FANTASIA

31.6
PASSENGER/SPACE RATIO

3.2
CREW/PASSENGER RATIO

TONNAGE	137.936
LENGTH/BEAM/DRAFT (IN METRES)	333.5/37.8/8.4
COMMISSIONED IN	2008
NUMBER OF PASSENGER DECKS	13
NUMBER OF PASSENGERS	4363
CREW	1370
NUMBER OF CABINS TOTAAL /YACHT CLUB	1637/71

MSC CRUISES
WWW.MSCYACHTCLUB.COM – WWW.MSCCRUISES.NL

NAUTICAL TERMS

Beaufort scale:
A system devised in 1805 by the British admiral, Sir Francis Beaufort, which measures the wind force on a scale of 0–12, based on observations of the effects of the wind. In 1874, the scale was adopted for international use. Later, the wind force was assigned a number and description according to the effect the wind had on the ocean surface. Sailors now estimate the wind force according to the appearance of the sea.

The Beaufort scale is subdivided as follows:

Wind force 0:
Calm, flat sea – wind speed is less than 1 knot.

Wind force 1:
Light air, – ripples without foam crests. Wind speed 1–3 knots.

Wind force 2:
Light breeze – small wavelets; crests of glassy appearance, not breaking. Wind speed 4–6 knots.

Wind force 3:
Gentle breeze – large wavelets; crests begin to break; scattered whitecaps. Wind speed 7–10 knots.

Wind force 4:
Moderate breeze – small waves with breaking crests; fairly frequent whitecaps. Wind speed 11–16 knots.

Wind force 5:
Fresh breeze – moderate waves of some length; many whitecaps; small amounts of spray. Wind speed 17–21 knots.

Wind force 6:
Strong breeze – Larger waves form; frequent foam crests; more spray. Wind speed 22–27 knots.

Wind force 7:
Near gale – high wind, moderate gale, sea heaps up. Some foam from breaking waves is blown into streaks along wind direction. Moderate amounts of spray. Wind speed 28–33 knots.

Wind force 8:
Gale, fresh gale – moderately high waves with breaking crests forming spindrift. Well-marked streaks of foam are blown along wind direction; considerable spray. Wind speed 34–40 knots.

Wind force 9:
Strong gale – high waves; crests sometimes roll over. Dense foam is blown along wind direction' large amounts of spray may begin to reduce visibility. Wind speed 41–47 knots.

Wind force 10:
Storm – whole gale; very high waves with overhanging crests; large patches of foam from wave crests give the sea a white appearance; considerable tumbling of waves with heavy impact. Large amounts of airborne spray that reduce visibility. Wind speed 48–55 knots.

Wind force 11:
Violent storm – exceptionally high waves; very large patches of foam, driven before the wind, cover much of the sea surface. Very large amounts of spray severely reduce visibility. Wind speed 56–63 knots.

Wind force 12:
Hurricane force – huge waves; sea is completely white with foam and spray. Air is filled with driving spray, greatly reducing visibility. Wind speed minimum 63 knots.

Bow:
The foremost part of a ship's hull extending into the prow.

Bridge:
Generally a raised cabin on a ship from where the captain gives his orders, the command and navigation centre. The bridge is manned at all times, also when the ship is in port.

Buoy:
Particular type of (usually floating) beacon for indicating a navigation route on rivers or on the sea.

Cabin:
A passenger's private room on board a ship.

Captain:
The commander of a ship, the highest position on board.

Captain's cocktail:
Welcome cocktail, normally on the second day of a cruise, during which the passengers can meet the captain and his staff. A festive event usually accompanied by special cocktails, champagne and snacks offered by the captain.

Captain's dinner:
Festive dinner at the end of a cruise when the captain dines together with the passengers. Some passengers have the privilege of being invited to dine at the captain's table. The captain does not generally eat in the same room as the passengers during a cruise.

Crew:
Staff working on a ship.

Crew/passenger ratio:
Indicates by way of a number the ratio between the passengers and the crew. The lower the number, the more staff there is on board.

Cruise Director:
The person responsible for the entertainment on board a cruise ship.

Drift:
Lateral movement of a ship due to the influence of currents or wind.

Galley:
The kitchen on board a ship.

Gross registered tonnage (or GRT):
See Ship's size.

Helm:
Wheel used to steer a vessel. Today, modern cruise ships are steered using a joystick.

Hotel Manager:
Officer in charge of passenger services.

Hull:
The main body of a ship, without the superstructure, masts and rigging.

Knot:
Speed in nautical miles per hour.

Lee:
Ship side away from the wind.

Logbook: See Ship's log.

Lower deck:
Deck under a ship's main deck.

Luffing:
Turning into the wind.

Marine telephone:
Radio transceiver device for communication between ships and between ships and shore-based stations.

Masthead light:
Forward shining white light, part of the navigation lights.

Mayday:
Mandatory call in marine radiotelephone communications when a ship is in distress (comparable to SOS in marine radiotelegraphy communication). 'Mayday' is a corruption of the French 'm'aidez', meaning 'Help me'.

Moor:
Tie up a ship.

Muster Station:
Assembly point on a ship where passengers assemble in the event of an accident or disaster.

Nautical chart:
Two-dimensional illustration of part of the earth's surface, including the sea and adjacent coastal area. On a sea chart, it must be easy to mark out the lubber line and it must be possible to measure the distance in nautical miles.

Nautical mile:
A distance of 1,852 metres (6,080 feet).

Net registered tonnage (NRT):
See Ship's size.

Passenger/space ratio or space ratio:
Indicates the space each passenger has on board. This figure is obtained by dividing the tonnage (ship's size) by the number of passengers it carries. The higher the ratio, the more space there is on the ship.

Pilot:
Specially trained helmsman with a good knowledge of local shallows who assists the captain when navigating into or out of a port.

Port:
The left-hand side of the ship when standing on a vessel and looking towards the prow.

Porthole:
Round casement window on board which is closed by means of clamps.

Prow:
Front end of a ship.

Purser:
The officer responsible for finances. This is also often the person passengers can approach with questions and complaints about the ship and everything concerning the voyage during their stay on board.

Radar:
Equipment that makes objects and obstacles on the water and along the waterfront visible on a screen by means of transmitting high-frequency signals.

Screw:
Blade-shaped propeller below the water line via which a ship is propelled.

Ship's log:
A 'diary' the captain is obliged to keep in which all details of a ship's passage (including the time spent in port) are recorded. The entries must be recorded in such a way that, the ship's route and/or any specific situations can be reconstructed, if necessary.

Ship's size:
Or tonnage, expressed in gross registered tonnage (GRT). One gross registered ton is 100 cubic feet (or 2.83 cubic metres). The term 'ton' comes from France and stood for a standard size of barrels in which wine was transported. A ship that could carry five of these barrels was therefore 5 tons in size. The calculation of the GRT includes all areas of a ship that are not accessible to the sea. The net registered tonnage is the part of the GRT designated for passengers. The NRT is obtained by subtracting the areas designated for propulsion, navigation, stores and crew accommodation from the GRT.

Side lights:
Green light on the starboard side and red light on the port side. These lights are part of the navigation lights.

Space ratio:
See Passenger space ratio

Stabilizer:
A device protruding from the hull below the water line which ensures stability under poor conditions when the ship is moving. A stabilizer can be retracted if conditions permit.

Staff Captain:
Or First Officer, the second in charge of a ship after the captain.

Starboard:
The right-hand side of the ship when standing on a vessel and looking towards the prow.

Stern:
Rear end of a ship.

Stern light:
Backward shining white light, part of the navigation lights.

Tender:
A small boat to transport passengers from the ship to shore and vice versa when the ship is not able to dock at the quayside.

Tonnage
See Ship's size

Windward:
Ship side facing the wind.

Zodiac:
Sturdy inflatable rubber dinghy with outboard motor used to take passengers ashore during excursions. A Zodiac can generally carry between 12-20 persons.

COLOPHON

www.lannoo.com

Register on our website to regularly receive our newsletter
with new publications as well as exclusive offers.

Texts
Iwein Maassen

Photography
Iwein Maassen
except page 22–27 & 139 (Silversea) / 94–97 (Windstar Cruises) /
192 & 194 b.r. (Cunard) / 229–235 (various).

Book design
Cedric Verhelst

Proofreading
Bracha De Man, Martin Lambert

Translation
Michael Lomax, Barry Stone

If you have any questions or remarks, please contact
our editorial team: redactiekunstenstijl@lannoo.com.

© Lannoo Publishers, Tielt, 2014
www.lannoo.com
Registration of copyright: D/2014/45/372 – NUR: 450
ISBN: 978 94 014 1149 3